M000194706

A Lyric Hammersmith Production

TERROR

A play by
Ferdinand von Schirach

Translated by David Tushingham

presented by arrangement with IPR Ltd, London,
in association with Kiepenheuer Buehnenvertriebs-GmbH, Berlin

First performed at the Lyric Hammersmith on
14 June 2017

The first production of *Terror* was performed on
3 October 2015 at Deutsches Theater, Berlin
and at the Schauspiel Frankfurt

TERROR

By Ferdinand von Schirach

Translated by David Tushingham

Cast *in alphabetical order*

Prosecuting Counsel Nelson	**Emma Fielding**
Christian Lauterbach	**John Lightbody**
Defence Counsel Biegler	**Forbes Masson**
Presiding Judge	**Tanya Moodie**
Franziska Meiser	**Shanaya Rafaat**
Lars Koch	**Ashley Zhangazha**

Creative Team

Directed by	**Sean Holmes**
Set Design by	**Anna Fleischle**
Costume Design by	**Loren Elstein**
Lighting by	**Joshua Carr**
Sound by	**Nick Manning**
Casting by	**Stuart Burt CDG**
Assistant Director	**Paloma Oakenfold**
Company Stage Manager	**Claire Bryan**
Deputy Stage Manager	**Helen King**
Assistant Stage Manager	**Lucy Holland**
Senior Producer	**Imogen Kinchin**
Producer	**Peter Holland**
Assistant Producer	**Sarah Georgeson**
Production Manager	**Seamus Benson**
Set Construction	**Clockwork Scenery**
Voting System by	**CLiKAPAD**
Costume Supervisor	**Ellen McQuaid**
Press Agency	**Jo Allan PR**
Marketing Design	**Stephen Long**

With thanks to
Lionel Digby at Flame Torbay, Tristram Kenton,
TEAfilms, Royal Exchange Theatre Manchester

Ferdinand von Schirach (Writer)

Ferdinand von Schirach is a German lawyer and writer.

Theatre includes: *Terror* (Deutsches Theater, Berlin/Schauspiel Frankfurt/national tour). It has since been staged in Austria, Denmark, Hungary, Japan, Poland, Switzerland, Turkey, the USA and Venezuela. Further openings are to follow in China, Greece, Israel, Italy, the Netherlands, Slovenia, Sweden and the Czech Republic.

Books include: *Crime*, *Guilt* and The *Collini Case*.

Short stories and essays include: *Carl Tohrberg's Christmas*, *The Girl Who Wasn't There* and *The Dignity is Violable*.

David Tushingham (Translator)

David Tushingham is a dramaturg and translator. He has worked extensively as a curator for European festivals including the Wiener Festwochen, the Ruhrtriennale, Theater der Welt and the Salzburg Festival, commissioning or co-commissioning works by artists as diverse as Forced Entertainment, Ivo van Hove, theatre-rites, Lemi Ponifasio/MAU and 1927.

As a dramaturg He has been responsible for such high profile world premieres as Simon Stephens's *Pornography*, directed by Sebastian Nübling (Deutsches Schauspielhaus in Hamburg/Festival Theaterformen), *The Book of Disquiet* by Michel van der Aa with Klaus Maria Brandauer (Linz 09) and *The Forbidden Zone* directed by Katie Mitchell with text by Duncan Macmillan (Salzburg Festival/Schaubühne Berlin).

As a translator He specializes in the work of contemporary German playwrights. His most recent translation of Roland Schimmelpfennig's *Winter Solstice* (ATC/Orange Tree) was a sell-out hit earlier this year. His other translations include *Idomeneus* (Gate), *The Golden Dragon*, *Jeff Koons* and *Arabian Night* (ATC), *The Woman Before*, *Mr Kolpert* and *Waiting Room Germany* (Royal Court), *Innocence* (Arcola), *Nordost* (Company of Angels), *Land Without Words* (Edinburgh) and *The Bitter Tears of Petra von Kant* (Southwark Playhouse). He has also adapted Salman Rushdie's *Haroun and the Sea of Stories* for the National Theatre.

Cast

Emma Fielding (Prosecuting Counsel Nelson)

Emma is an RSC Associate Artist.

Theatre credits include: *The Massive Tragedy of Madame Bovary* (Liverpool Everyman/Peepolykus); *Rapture Blister Burn* (Hampstead); *In the Republic of Happiness, Spinning into Butter* (Royal Court); *Decade* (Headlong); *The King's Speech* (Wyndham's); *Playing With Fire, Look Back in Anger, Arcadia* (National Theatre); *Rock 'n' Roll* (Duke of York's); *Macbeth, Heartbreak House, 1953, School For Wives* (Almeida); *Revolt She Said, Revolt Again, Cymbeline, Measure For Measure, The School for Scandal, Twelfth Night, A Midsummer Night's Dream, The Broken Heart* (RSC) and *Private Lives* (Albery/Richard Rogers, New York).

Film and television credits include: *Dark Angel, Close to the Enemy, Capital, Arthur and George, This Is England '90, DCI Banks, Silk, The Game, George Gently, The Suspicions of Mr Whicher, Kidnap and Ransom, Cranford, The Government Inspector, Waking the Dead, Other People's Children, A Respectable Trade, A Dance to the Music of Time, Drover's Gold, Poirot, Fast Girls, Discovery of Heaven* and *Pandaemonium*.

John Lightbody (Christian Lauterbach)

For the Lyric: *Three Sisters* (with Filter), *Ghost Stories* (Duke of York's), *A Midsummer Night's Dream* (with Filter, also Manchester Royal Exchange/Dublin Theatre Festival/Brisbane Festival).

Other theatre credits include: *Microcosm* (Soho); *Each His Own Wilderness* (Orange Tree); *Sixty-Six Books* (Bush); *Treasure Island* (Theatre Royal Haymarket); *The English Game* (Headlong); *Richard III* (Southwark Playhouse); *Jane Eyre* (Shared Experience); *Twelfth Night, A Doll's House* (West Yorkshire Playhouse); *The Taming of the Shrew, Measure for Measure, Richard III* (RSC); *Beautiful People* (Stephen Joseph); *A Christmas Carol, The Sea, Mansfield Park* (Chichester Festival Theatre); *As You Like It* (National Theatre); *Incarcerater* (Battersea Arts Centre) and *Romeo and Juliet* (Stray).

Film and television credits include: *Wallander, Agatha Raisin, EastEnders, Father Brown,The Musketeers, DCI Banks, The Mill, The Bletchley Circle, Holby City, Dalziel and Pascoe, Midsomer Murders, The Royal, The Flood, A Bunch of Amateurs, How to Lose Friends and Alienate People, Lady of Sorrows, Domestics* and *Maybe Baby*.

Forbes Masson (Defence Counsel Biegler)

Forbes is an RSC Associate Artist.

For the Lyric: *Dumbstruck* (Tron Theatre Production).

Other theatre credits include: *Travesties* (Apollo/Menier Chocolate Factory); *A Midsummer Night's Dream* (Theatre Royal Bath); *Dr Faustus* (Duke of York's); *Mr Foote's Other Leg* (Theatre Royal Haymarket);

A Midsummer Night's Dream (RSC/Garsington Opera); The Ruling Class, Richard III, Macbeth (Trafalgar Studios); Taming of the Shrew, As You Like It, Romeo and Juliet, Ahasverus, Tender Thing, Morte D' Arthur, The Histories, Twelfth Night, Comedy of Errors, Hamlet, Macbeth, The Grain Store (RSC); The Lion, the Witch and the Wardrobe (Kensington Gardens); King Lear (Headlong/Young Vic/Liverpool Everyman); ART, The Breathing House, STIFF! (Royal Lyceum Edinburgh); Trick is to Keep Breathing, The Real Wurld, Cinzano, Laurel and Hardy and Cinderella (Tron).

Film and television credits include: Catastrophe, Shetland, Doctors, Dead Boss, EastEnders, Young Person's Guide to Becoming a Rock Star, Monarch of the Glen, Hamish Macbeth, The High Life, My Dead Dad, Red Dwarf, Taggart, Rab C. Nesbitt and Victor and Barry.

Tanya Moodie (Presiding Judge)

For the Lyric: The Prince of Homburg (also RSC), The Under Room, The Chair Plays, A Thousand Stars Explode in the Sky.

Other theatre credits include: Trouble In Mind (Ustinov); Hamlet (RSC); Joanne (Soho); King John (Shakespeare's Globe); The House That Will Not Stand, The Piano Lesson (Tricycle); Intimate Apparel (Park); Fences (Duchess); Catch, ACDC, Fewer Emergencies, Incomplete and Random Acts of Kindness (Royal Court); The Overwhelming, The Darker Face of Earth, The Oedipus Plays (National Theatre); Sixty-Six Books (Bush); Trade, Peer Gynt, Coriolanus, Measure for Measure (RSC); Lysistrata (Arcola); A Doll's House, Medea (West Yorkshire Playhouse); The Vagina Monologues (The Arts/UK tour) and The School for Scandal (RSC).

Film and television credits include: Legacy, Rabbit Fever, The Tulse Luper Suitcases, The Final Passage, Skins, Sherlock, Lewis, The Body Farm, Holby City, The Street, The Clinic, Casualty, Sea of Souls, Silent Witness, Promoted to Glory, The Bill, Dr Willoughby, Maisie Raine and So Haunt Me.

Shanaya Rafaat (Franziska Meiser)

Theatre credits include: The White Devil (Shakespeare's Globe); A Tale of Two Cities (Royal and Derngate/UK Tour); Great Expectations (West Yorkshire Playhouse); Stateless (Tristan Bates); Around the World in 80 Days (St James); King Lear (Shakespeare's Globe/international tour); Twelfth Night (Lion and Unicorn); The Illusion (Southwark Playhouse); The Malcontent (White Bear); A Midsummer Night's Dream (RSC/Roundhouse/international tour); Judith, Sexual Perversity in Chicago, Blackbird 13, Hayavadana (National Centre for the Performing Arts, Mumbai) and The Maids (National Gallery of Modern Art, Mumbai).

Film and television credits include: EastEnders, Lewis, Silk, Schadenfreude, Complicit and Honeycomb Lodge.

Ashley Zhangazha (Lars Koch)

Theatre credits include: *The Lottery of Love* (Orange Tree); *Human Animals, Belong, Truth and Reconciliation* (Royal Court); *A Raisin in the Sun* (Sheffield Crucible/Eclipse); *Image of an Unknown Young Woman* (Gate); *Ah Wilderness!* (Young Vic); *Hamlet* (Royal Exchange); *Venice Preserv'd* (Spectator's Guild); *Henry V* (Michael Grandage Company/Noël Coward); *Fences* (Theatre Royal Bath/Duchess); *Macbeth* (Sheffield Crucible); *Richard II* (Donmar Warehouse); *King Lear* (Donmar Warehouse/BAM, New York) and *Danton's Death* (National Theatre).

Film and television credits include: *Victoria, Doctors, Humans* and *Ordinary Lies.*

Company

Sean Holmes (Director)

Sean is Artistic Director of the Lyric Hammersmith.

For the Lyric: *Shopping and F***ing, Bugsy Malone, A Midsummer Night's Dream* (with Filter, also UK tour/Manchester Royal Exchange/Dublin Theatre Festival/Brisbane Festival); *Herons,* Secret Theatre Shows 1, 2, 3, 5 and 7, *Cinderella, Desire Under the Elms, Morning, Have I None, Saved, Blasted* (winner Olivier Award 2011, Outstanding Achievement in an Affiliate Theatre), *A Thousand Stars Explode in the Sky, Ghost Stories* (also Duke of York's/Liverpool Playhouse/Panasonic Theatre, Toronto/Arts Theatre), *Three Sisters* and *Comedians.* In 2016 Sean directed *The Plough and the Stars* at the Abbey Theatre, Dublin (also Irish/US tour).

Sean was an Associate Director of the Oxford Stage Company from 2001 to 2006 and has also worked at the National Theatre, RSC, Tricycle, Royal Court, Donmar Warehouse, Chichester Festival Theatre and the Abbey Theatre, Dublin.

Anna Fleischle (Set Design)

Theatre credits include: *Everybody's Talking about Jamie* (Sheffield Crucible); *Rosencrantz and Guildenstern Are Dead* (The Old Vic); *Rent* (St James/UK tour); *Much Ado about Nothing, Troilus and Cressida* (Shakespeare's Globe); *Hangmen* (Wyndham's/Royal Court – Olivier Award for Best Set Design, Critics' Circle Award for Best Designer, Evening Standard Award for Best Design); *Don Juan in Soho* (Wyndham's); *Liberian Girl, The Kid Stays in the Picture* (Royal Court); *The Two Noble Kinsmen, Cymbeline, Love's Sacrifice* (RSC); *Don Giovanni* (WhatsOnStage Award for Best Opera Production), *Iphigenie en Tauride, –2.6 in Opera* (ETO); *John* for DV8 (National Theatre); *The End of Longing* (Playhouse); *Beware of Pity* (Schaubühne Berlin/Complicite, Barbican); *Can We Talk About This?* for DV8 (Sydney Opera House/National Theatre/International TourAustralian Helpmann Award for Best Ballet or Dance Work, Tanz Award for Production of the Year).

Loren Elstein (Costume Design)

Theatre credits include: *Love's Labour's Lost* (Royal Academy of Music); *Hidden* (UK tour); *The Ugly One* (Park); *Rosencrantz and Guildenstern Are Dead* (The Old Vic); *Rent* (*20th Anniversary Tour*, Michael Grandage Company); *Primetime* (Royal Court); *Stoneface* (Finborough); *The End of Longing* (Playhouse); *Wondrous Strange* (*RSC*); *A Room of Her Own* with *Mimbre Acrobats* (Southbank Centre/WOW Festival); *The Man Who Almost Killed Himself* (Edinburgh Festival); *A Midsummer Night's Dream* (Theater Trier); *Pia de Tolomei* (English Touring Opera) and *The Water Palace* (Tête à Tête Festival).

Film and Television credits include: Art Direction for *Magic FM*; FatBoy Slims *The Collection* and *Mcbusted's Most Excellent Adventure* tour music videos.

Joshua Carr (Lighting Design)

Theatre credits include: *Romeo and Juliet* (West Yorkshire Playhouse); *Everybody's Talking about Jamie* (Sheffield Theatres); *Sleeping Beauty*; *All My Sons*, *The Miser* (Watermill); *Stewart Lee: Content Provider* (London/ UK Tour); *Lunch*, *The Bow of Ulysses*, *RAZ* (Trafalgar Studios); *Wonderman* (Gagglebabble, National Theatre of Wales/Wales Millennium Centre); *Henry V* (Regent's Park Theatre); *Hangmen* (Royal Court/Wyndham's); *Dinner with Friends* (Park); *Albert Herring* (RCM); *The Dissidents* (Tricycle); *The Caucasian Chalk Circle* and *Britain's Best Recruiting Sergeant* (Unicorn); *The Wasp*, *In The Vale of Health* (Hampstead); *Exit the King* (Theatre Royal Bath); *Breeders* (St James); *Le Gateau Chocolat: Black* (Assembly Edinburgh/ Soho/Homotopia Festival, Liverpool/UK tour); *Yellow Face* (National Theatre/Park) and *Some Girl I Used to Know* (Arts/West Yorkshire Playhouse/UK tour).

Nick Manning (Sound Design)

Nick is Head of Sound at the Lyric Hammersmith.

For the Lyric: *Seventeen*, *Shopping and F***ing*, *Herons*, *Tipping the Velvet* Secret Theatre Company, *Ghost Stories* (also Duke of York's/Liverpool Playhouse/Panasonic Theatre, Toronto/Arts Theatre), *Metamorphosis* (also UK/international tour), *The Chair Plays*, *Morning*, *Saved*, Roald Dahl's *Twisted Tales* (also UK tour), *Comedians*, *The Birthday Party*, *The Resistible Rise of Arturo Ui*, *Beauty and the Beast*, *Absolute Beginners*, *The Odyssey*, *Girls Are Bigger Than Others*, *The Firework-Maker's Daughter*, *Oliver Twist*, *The Prince of Homburg* (also RSC) and *The Servant*.

Other theatre credits include: *I Capture the Castle* (Watford Palace/ Octagon Bolton/Kevin Wallace); *Happy Birthday Sunita* (Rifco/Watford Palace); *Mr Swallow – The Musical* (The Invisible Dot); *Candida* (Theatre Royal Bath); *Jumpers for Goalposts* (Paines Plough/UK tour); *The Acid Test* and *The Empire* (Royal Court).

Stuart Burt CDG (Casting)

Stuart was Head of Casting for the Ambassador Theatre Group until April 2017.

Theatre credits include: *Buried Child* (Trafalgar Studios); *The Spoils* (Trafalgar Studios); *The End of Longing, Women on the Verge of a Nervous Breakdown* (Playhouse); *Passion Play* (Duke of York's); *Blue/Orange, Private Lives, Gaslight, Dirty Rotten Scoundrels, The Rocky Horror Show, Annie Get Your Gun, Tonight's The Night, Spamalot* (UK tour) and *The Choir* (Glasgow Citizens/UK tour).

As Casting Director for The Jamie Lloyd Company: *Doctor Faustus* (Duke of York's); *The Maids, The Homecoming, The Ruling Class, Richard III, Macbeth* (Trafalgar Studios); *East is East, The Pride* (Trafalgar Studios/UK tour).

Stuart is a member of the Casting Director's Guild of Great Britain and Ireland.

Tipping the Velvet

Bugsy Malone

Herons

A Midsummer Night's Dream

Supported by

Registered Charity, No. 278518

Photography by Johan Persson and Tristram Kenton

The Lyric Hammersmith is one of the UK's leading producing theatres. For more than one hundred and twenty years it has been responsible for creating some of the UK's most adventurous and acclaimed theatrical work. It has gained a national reputation for its work with and for children and young people and creates pathways into the arts for young talent from all backgrounds, helping to diversify our industry. Recent productions include our critically acclaimed annual pantomimes, the smash hit *Bugsy Malone*, the international tour and co-production with Filter Theatre of *A Midsummer Night's Dream* and a new stage adaptation of Sarah Waters' *Tipping the Velvet*.

The Lyric's dual commitment to producing the highest quality contemporary theatre alongside nurturing the creativity of young people is what make it unique within the cultural ecology of the UK. It is a local theatre rooted in its community with a national and international reputation for the quality and innovation of its artistic work.

In April 2015 the Lyric reopened following a multi-million pound capital project, which saw the addition of the Reuben Foundation Wing housing state-of-the-art facilities for theatre, dance, film, music digital and more. The 'new' Lyric is now the largest creative hub in West London and home to an innovative partnership of like-minded leading arts organisations who work together to deliver life-changing creative opportunities for thousands of young West Londoners.

Artistic Director Sean Holmes
Executive Director Sian Alexander

For more information, please visit
lyric.co.uk

LYRIC HAMMERSMITH SUPPORTERS

Thank you to all our wonderful supporters who donate to the Lyric's work on and offstage. We couldn't do it without you.

LOVE THE LYRIC

Anonymous
Sian and Rob Alexander
Carrie and John Armstrong
Laura and John Banes
Lucy Bennell
Sherice Pitter
Guillaume and Carole Bonpun
Lisa Burger
The Callanan Family
Mike Dibb and Cheli Duran
Andrew and Lindsay Elder
Caroline Elliot
Liz Elston Mayhew and Luke Mayhew
Susannah Fancelli
Sadie Feast and Sean Holmes
Jane Fletcher
Kim Grant
Julian Granville and and Louisiana Lush
Lynne Guyton and Nick Dale
Lesley Hill and Russ Shaw
Ann Joseph
Juliet and Michael Humphries
Joanna Kennedy
Kate and Kevin McGrath
Catherine McKenna
John McVittie
Zhenya and Preston Mendenhall
Emma and Michael O'Kane
Marianne Rance
Peter Raymond
Janet Robb
Cathy Robertson
Tania Tate

INDIVIDUALS

Anonymous
Kate Brooke
Chris and Amanda Curry
Alex Joffe
Roger de Freitas
Livia and Colin Firth
Nick and Allison Gaynor
John and Clare Grumbar
David and Jammy Hoare
Sheila Clarke and Charles Gurassa
Sheelagh O'Neill
Sandy and Caroline Orr
Caroline Posnansky
Jon and NoraLee Sedmak
Sarah Jane Stubbs
Roger and Kate Wylie

TRUSTS and FOUNDATIONS

Andrew Lloyd Webber Foundation
Aziz Foundation
BBC Children in Need
British Council
Charles Hayward Foundation
The Daisy Trust
Discovery Foundation
Esmée Fairbairn Foundation
Fagus Anstruther Memorial Trust
Garfield Weston Foundation
Golsoncott Foundation
Hammersmith United Charities
The Idlewild Trust
The Ironmongers' Company
Jack Petchey Foundation
John Lyon's Charity
John Thaw Foundation
McGrath Charitable Trust
People's Postcode Trust
Reuben Foundation
Sam Griffiths Foundation
SHINE Trust
Sir John Cass's Foundation
The Tudor Trust
Wates Foundation
Winton Philanthropies
The Worshipful Company of Grocers

COMPANIES

Barclays
Bloomberg
HammersmithLondon
Horton and Garton
MAC
Piper Private Equity
UKTV
Hotel Partner – Novotel London West

Terror

Ferdinand von Schirach is a German lawyer and writer, who lives in Berlin. His story collections *Crime* and *Guilt* and novels *The Collini Case* and *The Girl Who Wasn't There* (*Tabu*) have been published in more than forty countries and sold millions of copies worldwide. The first production of *Terror* took place on the same evening in October 2015 at the Deutsches Theater in Berlin and the Schauspiel Frankfurt. It has since been staged in Austria, Denmark, Hungary, Japan, Poland, Switzerland, Turkey, the USA and Venezuela. Further openings are to follow in China, Greece, Israel, Italy, the Netherlands, Slovenia, Sweden and the Czech Republic.

David Tushingham is a dramaturg and translator who has worked extensively as a curator for European festivals including the Wiener Festwochen, the Ruhrtriennale, Theater der Welt and the Salzburg Festival. As a translator he specialises in the work of contemporary German playwrights, including Roland Schimmelpfennig, Dea Loher, Falk Richter and Rainald Goetz. He has also adapted Salman Rushdie's *Haroun and the Sea of Stories* for the National Theatre.

FERDINAND VON SCHIRACH

Terror

translated by

DAVID TUSHINGHAM

*with a speech by the author when presenting
the M100 Sanssouci Media Award 2015
to Charlie Hebdo*

FABER & FABER

First published in 2017
by Faber and Faber Limited
74–77 Great Russell Street, London WC1B 3DA

Typeset by Country Setting, Kingsdown, Kent CT14 8ES
Printed in England by CPI Group (UK) Ltd, Croydon CR0 4YY

Performing rights are represented by Gustav Kiepenheuer,
Bühnenvertriebs-GmbH, Berlin, Schweinfurthstr. 60,
D-14195 Berlin, Germany (info@kiepenheuer-medien.de),
and in the UK by International Performing Rights Ltd,
Top Floor, 3 Macroom Road, London W9 3HY
(info@iprltd.co.uk). No performance may be given
unless a licence has first been obtained

A CIP record for this book is available from the British Library

ISBN 978-0-571-34075-0

6 8 10 9 7 5

Terror was first performed in London at the Lyric Hammersmith on 14 June 2017. The cast, in alphabetical order, was as follows:

Prosecuting Counsel Nelson Emma Fielding
Christian Lauterbach John Lightbody
Defence Counsel Biegler Forbes Masson
Presiding Judge Tanya Moodie
Franziska Meiser Shanaya Rafaat
Lars Koch Ashley Zhangazha

Directed by Sean Holmes
Set design by Anna Fleischle
Costume design by Loren Elstein
Lighting by Joshua Carr
Sound by Nick Manning

*A map showing location of productions worldwide
together with the verdicts can be found at*
http://terror.theater/en

Characters

Presiding Judge

Lars Koch
Defendant

Biegler
Defence Counsel, male

Nelson
State Prosecutor, female

Christian Lauterbach

Franziska Meiser

Stenographer
female

Guard
male

This print edition of *Terror* is based on
the full, original German text and may differ
from the version used in performance.

TERROR

Prologue

The Presiding Judge enters. The curtain remains closed behind him. He is wearing a dark suit, a white shirt and a white tie. He is carrying his gown over one arm. He speaks directly to the audience.

Presiding Judge Good morning, ladies and gentlemen. I'm glad to see you all here on time. It's not easy parking round here and this building is a bit of a rabbit warren . . . Anyway, it's good that you've all managed to get here. Before we begin, I must ask you to forget everything that you have read or heard about this case. Yes, everything. It is you alone who have been called upon to judge this matter, you are the lay judges, the members of the public who today will sit in judgement on the defendant Lars Koch. The law grants you the power to determine the fate of a human being. Please take this responsibility seriously. You will judge solely what you hear in this courtroom. We lawyers describe this as 'evidence gained from within the hearing itself'. That means: only what is said by the defendant, the witnesses, the joint plaintiffs and legal experts in this courtroom, only the evidence which we gather here may provide the basis for your verdict. At the end of the trial you will be obliged to vote, and I shall announce the verdict that you have reached.

In court proceedings we re-enact the events: the court is a stage. Of course we're not going to perform a play, we're not actors. We will be re-enacting the events through language, this is our way of understanding them. And it's one that has stood the test of time. Hundreds of years ago the judges used to meet in a special place, one which was considered sacred, the thing. In those days to pronounce judgement meant to resolve disorder and restore order once again. Whenever harm was done – an attack by an enemy tribe for example – this was always the place where it would be discussed. Which woman was raped in the attack? Which hut was burnt to the ground? Which man was murdered? Our ancestors knew that in this way evil can lose its horror. Will we achieve that today? – I'm not sure. But we have to try. A judge does not regard anything as 'evil'. His – or her – verdicts are not hell and damnation but acquittal, prison or preventive detention.

So make your judgement calmly and in your own time. And above all: remember that before you there is a human being, someone who has the same dreams as you, the same needs. He too, just like you, is trying to find happiness. And that's why in your judgement you should retain your own humanity.

Now, I'd like to begin, but we're still waiting for the Counsel for the Defence – he's late.

The Guard approaches the Presiding Judge from the rear, says something to him quietly. The Presiding Judge nods. The Guard exits once again.

I've just been told he's finally arrived. So, let us begin.

The Presiding Judge exits, putting on his gown as he walks.

Act One

A courtroom. In the centre the judge's desk, with a Stenographer sitting on its right. The chair for the Presiding Judge is empty. To the left, beneath a window, sits the State Prosecutor with the joint plaintiff to her side and a little further back. The Counsel for the Defence is on the right. The Defendant is seated in a cell behind the Defence Counsel. In the centre, in front of the judge's desk, stand an empty chair and table for the witnesses.

The Guard sits on a stool next to the door. The State Prosecutor and the Stenographer wear black gowns, white blouses and white scarves. The Defendant has appeared in his Air Force uniform. The Guard wears the uniform of court officials for the state of Berlin. The Defence Counsel is not wearing a gown. The Presiding Judge enters the courtroom through a narrow door behind the judge's desk. At this point everyone on stage stands up.

Presiding Judge (*standing*) I declare this session of 16th division of the Criminal Court open. Please be seated.

The Presiding Judge sits down, followed by all the others. He waits until it is quiet.

For the record I confirm that the prosecution is represented by the State Prosecutor Ms Nelson, and Mr Biegler appears as Counsel for the Defence.

The defendant Major Lars Koch has been delivered here from custody. The court has therefore been assembled with all those present who were listed in the notice to appear. So far so good. Are there any questions or motions?

The State Prosecutor and Defence Counsel shake their heads.

Defence Counsel I would like Mr Koch to sit here next to me.

Presiding Judge Yes, I don't think he's a risk to anyone's safety.

He turns to the Guard.

Sergeant, would you please . . .

The Guard opens the cell door. The Defendant emerges and sits down next to the Defence Counsel.

(*To the Defendant.*) Good morning, Mr Koch. I will now take your personal details. Your first name please?

Defendant Lars.

Presiding Judge And your date of birth?

Defendant 14th March 1982. I'm thirty-one years old.

Presiding Judge Are you married?

Defendant Yes.

Presiding Judge Do you have any children from or outside of this marriage?

Defendant One son, Boris. He's two. No other children.

Presiding Judge And you live in Berlin?

Defendant Amselweg 56 in Steglitz.

Presiding Judge Mr Koch, you are a Major in the Air Force. You are currently being held in custody and have been relieved of your duties. Is that correct?

Defence Counsel My client's employer, the Air Force, is waiting for the outcome of this trial before deciding on his future.

Presiding Judge Thank you.

(*To the Stenographer.*) Personal details are the same as on page 159, Volume 1 of the main files.

The Stenographer writes down the personal details.

Does the court have any more questions about the defendant's personal details?

The State Prosecutor and Defence Counsel both shake their heads.

Fine. If there are no further motions or questions . . . I would ask the prosecution to read out the charge.

Defence Counsel Can we open a window? The air in here's terrible.

Presiding Judge You're right. We've had this problem for days. Apparently the ventilation system is broken, that's what the people in the office tell me. But if we open the window there's too much noise.

Defence Counsel From the street?

Presiding Judge It's so loud you can't even hear yourself think.

Defence Counsel I have enough trouble with that as it is.

Presiding Judge I beg your pardon?

Defence Counsel Never mind.

Presiding Judge But would you please put on your gown, Mr Biegler?

Defence Counsel Oh. I hadn't noticed. Rogues.

Presiding Judge Rogues? I don't understand you.

Defence Counsel The gown . . . You know. In 1726 Frederick William I declared that all lawyers were to wear dark gowns. His exact words were: 'So you can see the rogues coming from a long way off.'

Presiding Judge Aha.

Defence Counsel He had a point, the old King. Our colleagues are rather hard to take sometimes.

Presiding Judge Very well. Are you ready now, Mr Biegler?

Defence Counsel Yes.

Presiding Judge Then, if you please, State Prosecutor, the charge.

State Prosecutor (*standing*) Lars Koch, whose personal details have just been specified, is charged under the German Criminal Code according to section 154a, paragraph 1 of the Code of Criminal Procedure that on 26th May 2013 above the village of Oberappersdorf he did use deadly force to kill 164 people.

The charge states that on 26th May 2013 at 20:21 hours, using an air-to-air guided weapons system, he did shoot down a passenger aircraft type A320-100/200 manufactured by Airbus Industries belonging to Lufthansa German Airlines which was at that time flying from Berlin to Munich under flight code LH 2047, and did thereby kill the 164 persons on board. He is charged with the crime of murder according to section 211, paragraph 2, group 2, variant 3.52, paragraph 1 of the German Criminal Code.

Presiding Judge Thank you.

The charge has been referred unamended by a decision of the chamber on 28th February this year, on page 256 in Volume 6 of the main files.

(*To the Defendant.*) Mr Koch, in this trial you are accused of multiple murder. I am obliged to instruct you as the defendant that you may defend yourself by speaking or by being silent. You are not obliged to provide any testimony. If in the face of the charges raised against you you remain silent, the court cannot and shall not use your silence against you. Have you understood the charge and my instruction?

Defendant Yes.

Presiding Judge Very well. You will certainly have already discussed this with your Defence Counsel: at the preliminary proceedings you made a full confession. How do you wish to proceed today? Will you give testimony here?

Defendant (*stands*) I . . .

Defence Counsel pulls the Defendant by the sleeve back down on to his seat, and then stands up himself.

Defence Counsel I shall make a statement on behalf of the defendant.

Presiding Judge Fine. But you may remain seated.

Defence Counsel You know I prefer to stand. The dignity of the court . . .

Presiding Judge If it helps us get at the truth, very well.

Defence Counsel Ladies and gentlemen judges, every one of us knows where we were on 11th September 2001. Everyone knows where we saw those pictures for the first time – of the two planes which flew into the World Trade Center in New York, the third one which exploded by the Pentagon, and the fourth which crashed into a field near Pittsburgh. We can all see those people in front of us jumping to their deaths from a burning skyscraper. This was a terrorist act of mass murder. Eighteen months later a man here in Germany hijacked a light aircraft. He circled over Frankfurt and threatened to crash the plane into the headquarters of the European Central Bank.

This triggered a major security alert and Frankfurt city centre was evacuated. In the event everything ended peacefully, the man landed and offered no resistance to his arrest.

But we had learnt something from this incident: we had finally understood that we need to protect ourselves.

That is why in 2005 a new law was passed, the Aviation Security Act. Our parliament agreed that if the worst did happen, then the Minister of Defence would be entitled to use armed force. Even against a passenger plane with innocent people on board. In the most extreme case a hijacked aircraft could be shot down. A majority of members of parliament voted for this law. It allowed the state to kill people. Not people who have committed a crime but people who are the victims of crime. You can imagine how long those debates went on in parliament.

A year after it was passed, the most significant paragraphs of this legislation were revoked by the Federal Constitutional Court. The Federal Constitutional Court is our supreme court. All powers of the state are bound by its decisions. And this court decreed that it was unconstitutional to kill innocent people in order to save other innocent people. One life should never be weighed against another.

You, ladies and gentlemen, are the judges who have to come to a decision today. What happened is as follows. A terrorist hijacked a passenger plane. He wanted to crash it into a football stadium and kill 70,000 people. But one man – this man – had the courage and the power to act. He shot that plane down and all 164 people aboard died. That is the charge which has been brought. And the prosecution is correct: Lars Koch did do this. He killed the people on that plane, men, women and children. He weighed it up: the lives of 164 innocent people against the lives of 70,000 innocent people. Lars

Koch has admitted that he did this and we will do nothing to cover that up.

But, ladies and gentlemen, that is not the end of this trial, that is the beginning. There are 82 main files, 154 supplementary files, 46 folders of evidence, 15 files of photographs . . . All material relating to this case. My client has been in custody now for seven months, he has not seen his son in all that time, his wife is allowed to visit him once a fortnight for half an hour. But the only question in this case, the only question which you are being asked here today is: was Lars Koch permitted to kill these 164 people? Are there situations in our lives where it is right, proper and prudent to kill people? And indeed: where doing anything else would be absurd and even inhuman?

Of course such cases are so frightful as to make us question ourselves. But to believe that they do not exist because they are not allowed to exist – that is not only naive, it's dangerous. In fact it's very dangerous. There is no alternative: we have to accept that we live in a world where the most unimaginable and terrible things became reality a long time ago. We have to accept that there are limits to the principles of our constitution. And it is your job, ladies and gentlemen, as judges, your duty, to recognise this reality and to take account of it. I am confident that if you do so – do so fairly – that at the end of this trial you will find Lars Koch not guilty. You will find him not guilty because he acted. You will find him not guilty even though he killed 164 people.

Your Honour, Prosecutor, ladies and gentlemen judges: Lars Koch accepts the claims made in the charge. He admits that everything he is accused of happened exactly as it has been described. Yes, the facts are correct. But – and *this* but is the only thing that matters – it was not murder. The legal conclusions which the prosecution has drawn are wrong.

Presiding Judge Mr Koch, have I understood your Defence Counsel correctly: you accept the external series of events?

Defendant I beg your pardon?

Presiding Judge The facts. Are the facts correct of which you are accused in the charge?

Defendant Yes.

Presiding Judge Good. However, we would like to know more about the sequence of events. We would like to hear more from you about your motives. A blanket confession is insufficient.

Are you prepared to answer the questions of the court?

Defence Counsel My client will make no further statement at this point.

Presiding Judge What about later?

Defence Counsel We plan to do so, yes.

Presiding Judge Very well, as you wish, Counsel. Then let us begin hearing the evidence.

Sergeant, could you please see whether the witness Lauterbach has arrived?

Guard exits.

Guard (*calling outside*) Mr Christian Lauterbach . . .

Presiding Judge Prosecutor, Counsel, as you can see from the list, I have only called this one witness. Because the defendant has already admitted the deed in the preliminary proceedings, it seemed to me that we might dispense with any further witnesses. Of course we can add to the list if you consider this necessary once you've heard Mr Lauterbach's testimony. There will be no need for any formal motions. I will take a generous view of your proposals.

Defence Counsel That would be a first.

Presiding Judge What?

Defence Counsel You being generous.

Presiding Judge Excuse me?

Defence Counsel My client has been in custody for seven months. You could have released him: you know he's not a flight risk. You really can't talk about being generous.

Presiding Judge I can't release someone who's accused of murdering 164 people.

Defence Counsel You could – you just don't want to . . .

State Prosecutor Gentlemen, please.

Defence Counsel This isn't about saying please.

Presiding Judge You're being rude, Mr Biegler.

Defence Counsel It's not about manners either. Being a defence lawyer is not a popularity contest.

The Guard and Lauterbach enter. Lauterbach walks to the witness's chair, which is pointed out to him by the Presiding Judge. He sits down.

Presiding Judge Good morning. You are Christian Lauterbach?

Lauterbach Yes, good morning.

Presiding Judge Mr Lauterbach, I have to start by instructing you as a witness that you are obliged to tell the truth here. You may add nothing and omit nothing. The punishments for false testimony are severe. You can be required to take an oath regarding your statement. Do you understand?

Lauterbach Yes.

Presiding Judge (*to Stenographer*) Instruction completed.

The Stenographer stamps the record accordingly.

Please state your personal details for the record.

Lauterbach My name is Christian Georg Lauterbach.

The Stenographer takes down his personal details.

Presiding Judge Speak up a little, please.

Lauterbach Yes.

Presiding Judge And you go by the name of Christian?

Lauterbach Yes.

Presiding Judge Your age last birthday please.

Lauterbach I'm forty-nine.

Presiding Judge Where do you live?

Lauterbach In Goch. It's on the Lower Rhine.

Presiding Judge Are you related to the defendant either by birth or marriage?

Lauterbach No.

Presiding Judge Your profession?

Lauterbach Soldier.

Presiding Judge And rank?

Lauterbach Lieutenant Colonel.

Presiding Judge Thank you very much.

We have a form here from the Air Force giving their permission for you to testify. According to this you may refuse to ask answer any questions relating to state secrets. Is that correct?

Lauterbach That is the case.

Presiding Judge In the event that I or anyone else in the courtroom asks you in the course of this hearing about any state secrets and you are not permitted to answer those questions, you must draw that to our attention. You are not allowed simply to give evasive answers. Do you understand this too?

Lauterbach Yes.

Presiding Judge We are concerned with 26th May last year. Please describe the events of that day from your personal point of view.

Lauterbach I was on the duty rota as DC from 1400 hours. That's the second shift.

Presiding Judge DC?

Lauterbach Duty Controller.

Presiding Judge As a matter of principle, Mr Lauterbach: we are in a courtroom here and not in the Air Force. The lay judges have not read the files and we are not all familiar with your terminology. You're going to have to explain all these military terms to us. What is the task of a Duty Controller?

Lauterbach The DC is an Air Force staff officer. Do you want me to go into the technicalities?

Presiding Judge Please do.

Lauterbach German airspace is supervised by NATO. The entire air defence system is under their control. However, if an aeroplane is hijacked in German airspace, NATO's jurisdiction ends and command is transferred to the so-called National Airspace Security Situation and Command Centre.

Presiding Judge Complicated.

Lauterbach In future it's planned to bring everything together under one European agency, but we haven't got that far yet.

Presiding Judge I see. So normally NATO watches over our airspace but the national defence system is activated for hijackings.

Lauterbach You can put it that way, yes.

Presiding Judge Who is employed at this command centre?

Lauterbach Staff from the Ministry of Defence, in other words Air Force personnel. They have many years' experience monitoring airspace.

Presiding Judge And apart from them?

Lauterbach There are also officials from the Ministry of the Interior, Ministry of Transport, Construction and Urban Development and the Federal Office of Civil Protection and Disaster Assistance.

Presiding Judge How many people altogether?

Lauterbach Between sixty and sixty-five.

Presiding Judge And where is this command centre located?

Lauterbach In Uedem in North Rhine-Westphalia. Along with the NATO Combined Air Operations Centre.

Presiding Judge And that's where you were on duty on 26th May?

Lauterbach Yes.

Presiding Judge Could you please explain to us precisely how airspace is monitored?

Lauterbach We use both primary and secondary radar. And we also have access to all the data from civil aviation security and state and federal police. We also receive any secret service information relevant to air traffic. All of this is collated to give us an overview of the situation.

Presiding Judge I see.

Lauterbach We're constantly on the lookout for Renegade.

Presiding Judge Renegade?

Lauterbach Sorry. That refers to a civilian aircraft being pirated in the air for terrorist purposes. We call that 'Renegade'.

Presiding Judge It sounds American.

Lauterbach It is. It's the internationally accepted term.

Presiding Judge Very well then, Renegade. How do you find out about such a case?

Lauterbach That is the most difficult part of our job. What we do is stay in radio contact with every aircraft and look for irregularities.

Presiding Judge Such as?

Lauterbach An aeroplane going off course or the automatic recognition system being switched off or simply being unable to make radio contact.

Presiding Judge Does that happen often?

Lauterbach Usually three or four times a day. They're hardly ever hijackings. Still, we need to check on every single one and then make a decision.

Presiding Judge I see.

Lauterbach On 26th May it was very straightforward, though.

Presiding Judge Straightforward? Why?

Lauterbach The terrorist forced the pilot to announce over the radio that he had hijacked the aeroplane.

Presiding Judge Could you be more precise, please?

Lauterbach At 19:32 we received a radio transmission from Lufthansa flight LH 2047. This was the flight from Berlin-Tegel to Munich, departing 19:20, landing 20:30. The pilot said he was being forced to read a text aloud.

Presiding Judge What was this text?

Lauterbach (*reads from a sheet of paper*) 'With the grace of God, I have this plane in my power. Rejoice, community of Muslims. The crusader governments of Germany, Italy, Denmark and England have killed our brothers, now we will kill your families. You shall die as we have died.'

Presiding Judge In those precise words?

Lauterbach Yes, those were the words.
    Then the pilot said that the terrorist wanted to crash the aircraft into the football stadium in Munich. He was referring to the Allianz Arena. That day there was an international match there: Germany versus England. The stadium was sold out, 70,000 spectators.

Presiding Judge You heard him say that on the radio yourself?

Lauterbach Yes. It's recorded, all radio transmissions are saved. I put it on loudspeaker so that everyone in the room could hear.

Presiding Judge Did the terrorist reveal his identity?

Lauterbach We only found that out later. He was a suicide bomber belonging to an Al Qaeda splinter organisation.

Presiding Judge That's not something you know from your own enquiries, is it?

Lauterbach No, from the Federal Criminal Police. And then the newspapers. As I said, that wasn't till much later.

Presiding Judge What did you do after you'd heard what was said on the radio?

Lauterbach I informed everyone in the room.

Presiding Judge Yes, you put the message on the loudspeakers, you've already said that. I mean after that.

Lauterbach Right. I initiated a sequence of calls to all NATO command centres. At the same time I informed the Commander of the Air Force, Lieutentant General Radtke.

Presiding Judge Who is he?

Lauterbach He is the most senior general in the Air Force. I reported to him.

Presiding Judge Is that usual practice?

Lauterbach Yes, and it's in the official regulations.

Presiding Judge Go on.

Lauterbach I gave the order for the rapid reaction force to be deployed and to establish visual contact with the hijacked Lufthansa aeroplane.

Presiding Judge What is a rapid reaction force?

Lauterbach Two fighter aircraft, of the Eurofighter type. They are on constant standby. One unit is stationed in the north, in Wittmund in East Frisia, and the other is in the south, in Neuburg on the Danube. The fighters from Wittmund were airborne at the time. It took the pilots eleven minutes to reach the Lufthansa plane.

Presiding Judge That's very fast, isn't it?

Lauterbach It's normal. Our airspace isn't that big.

Presiding Judge Fine. Who were the pilots? I mean the pilots of the rapid reaction force.

Lauterbach Major Koch and First Lieutenant Weinberger.
   The rapid reaction force is generally staffed so that an older, more experienced pilot will fly together with a younger one. Major Koch is thirty-one years old, First Lieutenant Weinberger twenty-five.

Presiding Judge I see. Let's go back to your telephone call with Lieutenant General Radtke.

Lauterbach Yes.

Presiding Judge What were his orders?

Lauterbach The first thing General Radtke wanted to know was whether the rapid reaction force already had visual contact with the pilot.

Presiding Judge What was your answer?

Lauterbach After the fighters had caught up with the Lufthansa aircraft, it was possible to establish visual contact. The officers reported being able to see a man dressed in civilian clothes in the cockpit. This man was between the pilot and co-pilot. Radio contact was no longer possible as the devices on board the Lufthansa aircraft had been switched off.

Presiding Judge And that's what you passed on?

Lauterbach Of course.

Presiding Judge What were Radtke's orders then?

Lauterbach To divert the Lufthansa aircraft off course and force it to land.

Presiding Judge What exactly did he say to you?

Lauterbach 'Intervention.' The order was 'Intervention'. That means forcing it off course.

Presiding Judge Intervention, I see.

Lauterbach Yes. At the same time all the staff in the control centre were looking for an airfield to make a landing. We have contingency plans at certain airfields for cases like this.

Presiding Judge So you passed on the order.

Lauterbach Yes, immediately.

Presiding Judge Just that one word?

Lauterbach Yes. Military language is concise. There was no need for more.

Presiding Judge But as far as I can tell from the files, the Lufthansa plane did not react.

Lauterbach That's right, it maintained its course.

Presiding Judge What happened next?

Lauterbach I reported this to General Radtke. And I gave him the additional details.

Presiding Judge What details?

Lauterbach That we were dealing with a Lufthansa aircraft of the Airbus A320-100/200 type. That in addition to the terrorist there were 164 people on board. How many of those belonged to the crew. Its speed. Its estimated time of impact. Those sort of things. Details.

Presiding Judge And where had you got these details from?

Lauterbach From my colleagues in civil aviation security. There were 98 men, 62 women and two children. I had the passenger list in front of me. The youngest child was just four years old, a girl.

Presiding Judge Excuse me? I couldn't hear you.

Lauterbach I said one of the children was just four years old.

Presiding Judge Yes, well. What orders did you receive from General Radtke?

Lauterbach It took about six minutes. In a case like this General Radtke has to call the Minister of Defence and inform him of the situation. At the same time he is in contact with the Military Supreme Commander. General Radtke made the Minister of Defence a proposal: that is his duty. The Minister then decides whether he is going to follow this proposal. That is what's written in the Aviation Security Law and in the official regulations.

Presiding Judge What did General Radtke propose?

Lauterbach For cases like this there's a series of steps laid down in advance.

Presiding Judge Oh. And they are?

Lauterbach Step one: divert the plane. Step two: warning shots.

Presiding Judge That means?

Lauterbach The Minister orders the unit to fire warning shots.

Presiding Judge Can't the pilots decide that for themselves?

Lauterbach To fire warning shots?

Presiding Judge Yes.

Lauterbach No, only the Minister is allowed to do that.

Presiding Judge Very well, then. Warning shots. Did you receive this order? That the pilots should now fire warning shots?

Lauterbach Yes.

Presiding Judge What happens there? These warning shots, I mean.

Lauterbach That's going to get technical now, Your Honour.

Presiding Judge Explain anyway. We'll do our best to follow.

Lauterbach The Eurofighter is equipped with a single-barrel gas-operated five-chamber revolver cannon made by Mauser. The weapon is mounted in the right wing. Its rate of fire is 1,700 rounds per minute, travelling at a velocity of 1,025 metres per second. Which means over four kilogrammes of ammunition is fired in 0.5 seconds. It has a range of around 1,600 metres. For airborne targets it is usually loaded with high explosive ammunition.

Presiding Judge Aha.

Lauterbach I passed the order on to the rapid reaction force. 'Warning burst', that's what we call it. In military language, I mean.

Presiding Judge Who was it fired these shots?

Lauterbach Major Koch. He released a burst of fire from the on-board cannon. It's a mixed load: tracers and conventional ammunition.

Presiding Judge Did you decide who would fire the shots?

Lauterbach No, the pilots decide that themselves. But it is customary for the senior officer to do so.

Presiding Judge The defendant, in other words.

Lauterbach That's right.

31

Presiding Judge And what happened next? Would the captain of a civilian aircraft even notice the warning shots?

Lauterbach Of course. He can see the gun smoke and hear the shots. And he can see the path of the tracer bullets.

Presiding Judge Was there a reaction of any kind?

Lauterbach No. And if I may say so, warning shots like these are pretty damned impressive. It takes quite a lot not to react to them.

Presiding Judge I see. In your military experience are there any other ways of interrupting a flight?

Lauterbach You mean other than warning shots and diversion?

Presiding Judge Yes.

Lauterbach I'm afraid not.

Presiding Judge You're afraid not.

Lauterbach Anyone else would say the same.

Presiding Judge What did you do next?

Lauterbach I reported back to General Radtke again.

Presiding Judge And then?

Lauterbach General Radtke took a couple of minutes to reply. During that time he had proposed to the Minister of Defence that the Lufthansa aircraft be shot down.

Presiding Judge And?

Lauterbach That is the final step. But the Minister of Defence rejected it.

Presiding Judge How do you know that?

Lauterbach The General told me.

Presiding Judge Did Radtke make any comment on the Minister's decision?

Lauterbach What do you mean?

Presiding Judge Well, for example did he say, 'Unfortunately he rejected it'? Or something like that?

Lauterbach No.

Presiding Judge Had you expected that to be the Minister's decision?

Lauterbach Yes. We all know the views of the Federal Constitutional Court.

Presiding Judge You mean the ruling which declared part of the Aviation Security Law to be unconstitutional?

Lauterbach Yes. At the time everyone in the team had talked about it.

Presiding Judge Very well. You passed that decision on to the pilots.

Lauterbach What?

Presiding Judge That they weren't allowed to shoot.

Lauterbach Yes, of course.

Presiding Judge And what happened then?

Lauterbach Nothing.

Presiding Judge Nothing? I don't understand.

Lauterbach Well, we just stared at the screens, there was nothing else we could do. Everyone was hoping for a miracle, I was at any rate.

Presiding Judge Did you question the General's order or did you simply pass it on to the rapid reaction force?

Lauterbach It's not my job to question orders.

Presiding Judge So you passed on the instructions exactly as you received them?

Lauterbach Yes.

Presiding Judge I see. I am trying to imagine the situation. You are now looking at the screens and waiting. How long did that go on, approximately?

Lauterbach Twenty-eight minutes.

Presiding Judge That long?

Lauterbach Yes.

Presiding Judge So almost half an hour.

Lauterbach Yes.

Presiding Judge And then?

Lauterbach Major Koch –

Presiding Judge The defendant?

Lauterbach He asked twice whether he had understood everything correctly.

Presiding Judge The order that he was not allowed to shoot?

Lauterbach Correct. The order to shoot the aircraft down is 'engage'. I confirmed to him both times that no such order had been given.

Presiding Judge Did you have a clear connection? Could the defendant understand you properly?

Lauterbach Yes, he repeated it himself.
I'm sorry, could I have a glass of water please?

Presiding Judge Sergeant, a glass of water please for the witness.

The Guard brings a carafe of water and a glass.

Lauterbach Thank you.

He pours himself a glass of water and drinks.

Presiding Judge Are you ready to continue?

Lauterbach Yes.

Presiding Judge Good. So the defendant asked twice. Then what happened?

Lauterbach The next thing was Major Koch reported that the Lufthansa aircraft had begun its descent. This was confirmed by what I saw on my screen.

Presiding Judge How far away were the planes from the stadium?

Lauterbach Around twenty-five kilometres.

Presiding Judge Had the Lufthansa aircraft changed its course at all during the entire time?

Lauterbach No. Then Major Koch shouted into the microphone.

Presiding Judge He shouted?

Lauterbach Yes.

Presiding Judge What did he shout?

Lauterbach 'If I don't shoot now, thousands of people are going to die.'

Presiding Judge Were those his exact words?

Lauterbach Yes.

Presiding Judge And then?

Lauterbach I saw on my screen that Major Koch had fired the Sidewinder.

Presiding Judge And what is a Sidewinder?

Lauterbach A munition.

Presiding Judge Presumably things are about to get technical again?

Lauterbach It's an air-to-air guided missile type AIM-9L/I Sidewinder.

Presiding Judge And how does it work?

Lauterbach The Sidewinder has an infrared sensor. It homes in on heat sources.

Presiding Judge And that is exactly what happened?

Lauterbach The heat-seeker locked on to and hit the right engine of the Lufthansa aircraft. The plane crashed into a potato field.

Presiding Judge What time was that?

Lauterbach 20:21. Wait a moment, let me just check.
Yes, at precisely 20:21 hours and 34 seconds. That was the moment when the Sidewinder was released electronically.

Presiding Judge And the rapid reaction force?

Lauterbach The two fighters turned away and flew back to base. Major Koch was arrested as soon as he'd landed. Our colleagues from the Federal Police had of course called out the emergency services. They searched the wreckage for survivors and secured the scene. There were no survivors.
But I only know that second hand.

Presiding Judge Did you have any means of preventing the weapon from being fired from the command centre?

Lauterbach How?

Presiding Judge I don't know, blocking it by radio perhaps.

Lauterbach No, there's no way of doing that. The pilot can and must have independent control of his own weapons system.

Presiding Judge That makes sense. So the matter lay exclusively in his hands.

Lauterbach Yes.

Presiding Judge And the planes are always armed?

Lauterbach They're fighter jets. Of course they're armed.

Presiding Judge Did you report to General Radtke that the plane had been shot down?

Lauterbach Of course.

Presiding Judge How did he react?

Lauterbach Not at all.

Presiding Judge I beg your pardon?

Lauterbach He simply received the message. What was going on inside him, I don't know. He did, however, order that all recordings of the incident should be secured and that Major Koch should be handed over to the Federal Police. Without delay.

Presiding Judge Yes. Well. For my part I have no further questions for the witness. The facts of the case appear to lie clearly before us. They confirm the defendant's confession on every single point. Does anyone else in the court have questions for the witness? Prosecutor?

State Prosecutor I have no questions for the witness.

Presiding Judge Counsel for the Defence, any questions?

Defence Counsel No, I don't have any questions either.

Presiding Judge Fine. Are there any motions to place the witness under oath? If not, then . . .

State Prosecutor I do have a question after all. Sorry.

Presiding Judge Yes, of course.

State Prosecutor Mr Lauterbach, just very briefly: at the beginning of your testimony you said that everyone in the room knew that the plane had been hijacked.

Lauterbach Yes.

State Prosecutor You said that among you there were officals of the Federal Police, the Ministry of the Interior, the Ministry of Transport, Disaster Assistance and so forth.

Lauterbach That is correct.

State Prosecutor Who in the room decided to evacuate the stadium?

Lauterbach Evacuate the stadium?

State Prosecutor Yes, who ordered that?

Lauterbach I don't know.

State Prosecutor Try to remember, please. We've got time.

Lauterbach I've no idea.

State Prosecutor Really?

Lauterbach I honestly don't know.

State Prosecutor You're in the same position as me, then: I don't know either. And do you know, Mr Lauterbach, do you know why I don't know?

Lauterbach No.

State Prosecutor The reason I don't know is because nobody did make that decision. No one. Not a single person in your command centre gave the order to clear the stadium at any time.

Lauterbach But . . .

State Prosecutor Yes?
  Now the question I have is a very simple one: Why not? Why was that order not given?
  Mr Lauterbach?

Lauterbach Yes . . .

State Prosecutor We're waiting . . .

Lauterbach I . . . we . . . we didn't have time for that.

State Prosecutor Really?

Lauterbach Yes.

State Prosecutor So there was no time. If I look here at the timings which you have given us, then from the first radio signal – at 19:32 – to the estimated impact of the aircraft – at 20:24 – there was time. Fifty-two minutes of time, to be precise.

Lauterbach Fifty-two minutes . . .

State Prosecutor Yes. Fifty-two minutes.
  I have here in front of me the emergency plan for the stadium. Page 438 from Volume 19. According to this, at full capacity the entire stadium can be evacuated completely within fifteen minutes. In fifty-two minutes therefore all or most probably almost all of those people would have been able to leave the stadium.

Lauterbach All of them.

State Prosecutor There's no need to repeat everything I say. I just want to know why nobody ordered the stadium to be cleared.

Lauterbach That . . . that . . .

State Prosecutor Was it perhaps the case that you and your colleagues were quite simply certain?

Lauterbach Certain? Certain about what?

State Prosecutor Certain that Major Koch would shoot the plane down.

Lauterbach No.

State Prosecutor I'll ask you again: was it not the case that the only reason you did not evacuate the stadium was because you knew that if the worst came to the worst the defendant would shoot?

Lauterbach No.

State Prosecutor No? Think again before you answer. You can be put on oath here – as the Presiding Judge has already reminded you.

Lauterbach Yes, possibly.

Presiding Judge Speak up a little please. The acoustics in this room are very poor.

Lauterbach I could imagine that.

State Prosecutor What exactly could you imagine?

Lauterbach That Major Koch would shoot.

State Prosecutor And why could you imagine that, Mr Lauterbach?

Lauterbach Because . . .

State Prosecutor Could it possibly be because you yourself would also have shot the plane down?

Lauterbach No, I don't know . . .
    (*To the Presiding Judge.*) Do I have to answer that question?

40

Presiding Judge Well, I can't see how you might incriminate yourself by giving a truthful answer.

Lauterbach What?

Presiding Judge You do have to answer the question.

Lauterbach (*to the State Prosecutor*) I don't know.

State Prosecutor Perhaps I can help you, Mr Lauterbach. Are you aware that the Minister of Defence at the time of the Federal Constitutional Court's ruling said he would still order hijacked planes to be shot down?

Lauterbach Hmm.

State Prosecutor Yes or no?

Lauterbach I am aware of that remark, yes.

State Prosecutor Defence Minister Jung said, and I quote: 'In the interim period we would intervene by declaring an extra-legal state of emergency.'

Lauterbach Yes, I did read that.

State Prosecutor Was that discussed within the team?

Lauterbach Of course. It was the topic of discussion.

State Prosecutor The topic of discussion?

Lauterbach Everyone in this unit is constantly thinking about what is going to happen in the event of Renegade.

State Prosecutor And do you also remember the Defence Minister saying that the only pilots who would be selected were those prepared to shoot down a plane in an emergency?

Lauterbach I am also aware of that.

State Prosecutor So was that ultimately the reason? Was that why no one thought of evacuating the stadium?

Lauterbach shakes his head.

Think this through one more time. You were sure how Major Koch would react, weren't you?

Lauterbach I don't know what to say. I'm not prepared for that question.

Presiding Judge The truth would be helpful.

Lauterbach I . . . assume that most of my colleagues would act precisely as Major Koch did. Yes. I too would probably have shot down the Lufthansa aircraft.

State Prosecutor There we are.

Lauterbach What are you getting at?

State Prosecutor So not evacuating the stadium was a gamble, Mr Lauterbach.

Lauterbach I beg your pardon?

State Prosecutor You were gambling. You gambled the lives of 70,000 people on the defendant's decision.

Lauterbach That's cynical.

State Prosecutor Cynical? Why is it cynical?

Lauterbach I assure you I was not gambling.

State Prosecutor Mr Lauterbach, if you had had the stadium cleared, none of the spectators would have been in danger. But evidently you didn't want to do that.

Lauterbach For God's sake – I didn't want to do that?

State Prosecutor Yes, if we're being honest, at that point you were certain that things would turn out differently. That the defendant would shoot. And that is precisely the gamble you took.

Lauterbach I can only repeat . . .

State Prosecutor There's no need. It's already clear: it wasn't a calculation, 164 lives against 70,000 lives . . .

Defence Counsel That is enough. The witness here is not the accused. I move . . .

State Prosecutor I'll put it another way. Mr Lauterbach, imagine there was no rapid reaction force.

Lauterbach This is getting confusing now.

State Prosecutor Just imagine that for a moment.

Lauterbach Yes.

State Prosecutor All you had was the terrorist's words on the radio. What would you have done then?

Lauterbach I don't know . . .
Now I understand. You think someone would have –

State Prosecutor – ordered –

Lauterbach – the stadium to be cleared.
But that's a completely different situation.

State Prosecutor Is it?

Lauterbach I mean . . . I think . . .

State Prosecutor Thank you. No further questions.

Presiding Judge Counsel, do you have any questions?

Defence Counsel Only three.

Presiding Judge Go ahead.

Defence Counsel Were you personally responsible for evacuating the stadium?

Lauterbach No, that was the Bavarian emergency services.

Defence Counsel Was the defendant responsible for evacuating the stadium?

Lauterbach Of course not.

Defence Counsel The stadium was full as the Lufthansa aircraft approached. Could the defendant do anything to change that

Lauterbach No.

Defence Counsel Thank you. That should be made clear. No further questions.

Presiding Judge Very well. Are there any motions to place the witness under oath?

> *Both State Prosecutor and Defence Counsel shake their heads.*

(*To Lauterbach.*) Then you are discharged as a witness, Mr Lauterbach. The court thanks you for your testimony.

Lauterbach Excuse me, but where do I hand in the form for witness compensation? Today's my day off.

Presiding Judge Come here. Let me see that.

> *Lauterbach goes to the judge's desk and hands the Presiding Judge a form. The Presiding Judge skims through it, looks at the clock on the courtroom wall, signs it and hands it back to Lauterbach.*

There you are.

Lauterbach Thank you.

Presiding Judge Take that to room 332b, it's down the corridor, the fourth door.

Lauterbach Thank you very much.

> *Lauterbach exits.*

Presiding Judge Now, Counsel, is your client prepared to answer further questions from the court?

Defence Counsel Yes.

Presiding Judge Mr Koch?

Defendant I'll try.

Presiding Judge Good, then please step forward and take the witness's chair. It will be easier to hear you that way.

The Defendant walks up to the witness's chair and sits down.

Of course you may pause in your answers at any point to speak to your Defence Counsel.

Defendant Fine.

Presiding Judge We will start with some biographical details, Mr Koch. You are your parents' first child?

Defendant Yes, I have one sister who is three years younger.

Presiding Judge What were your parents' professions?

Defendant My father was also in the Air Force. After reunification he became a staff officer in the press department at the Ministry of Defence. My mother is a bookseller. After I was born, she stayed at home. She was a housewife and mother.

Presiding Judge You were born in Freiburg and attended school there?

Defendant Yes, kindergarten, primary school and grammar school, all in Freiburg.

Presiding Judge I have your school-leaving certificate here. You attained the top grade in every subject. Your class teacher adds that in Mathematics you even got the highest mark in the state of Baden-Württemberg.

Defendant That is correct.

Presiding Judge What were your interests outside of school?

Defendant Physics. Every year I used to enter 'Young Scientist of the Year'.

Presiding Judge And one time you even won second prize.

Defendant Yes. Apart from that I did a lot of sport, especially football and athletics.

Presiding Judge Would it be fair to say that school and learning came easily to you?

Defendant Yes.

Presiding Judge Your childhood and youth were untroubled?

Defendant I would say they were happy. Yes.

Presiding Judge Let us come to your choice of profession. Was it actually your own wish to become a soldier? Or was it your father's?

Defendant It's true that my father did also want to be a fighter pilot.

Presiding Judge And?

Defendant He didn't make it.

Presiding Judge I see.

Defendant I always wanted to join the Air Force. When I was a child I wanted to be a fighter pilot. It was all I was interested in. I used to have posters of aeroplanes on my bedroom wall.

Presiding Judge What made you interested in them?

Defendant I found it fascinating. The dream of flying, the speed, the precision of the planes.

Presiding Judge As soon as you left school, when you were eighteen, you applied for a position as an officer trainee . . .

Defendant I was invited to attend the Officer Candidate Assessment Centre in Cologne and took an aptitude test. That lasted two days. Afterwards I was examined to check that I was medically and psychologically fit and had the psychomotor skills necessary for the service. In October I entered the service at Fürstenfeldbruck.

Presiding Judge What did that consist of?

Defendant In the first year I completed officer training and was commissioned with the rank of Ensign. Then over the next two years I went through basic and advanced training as a pilot.

Presiding Judge Where did you do that?

Defendant In the United States, to be precise in Goodyear, Arizona. Then I trained as a jet pilot at Sheppard Air Force Base in Texas. Fifteen months.

Presiding Judge What does one learn there?

Defendant Essentially: flying.
There is theoretical and simulator-based training for about three hundred flying hours. Once that section of the training is completed, you are licensed to fly military aircraft.

Presiding Judge And then?

Defendant Then I had to familiarise myself with flying conditions in Germany.

Presiding Judge Are they so very different?

Defendant The topography and weather conditions are different. And it's much more complicated moving around within European airspace – if you think of how many borders there are and the number of flights here.

Presiding Judge I see. Did you sign up for sixteen years as a regular soldier right at the start?

Defendant The term of duty is not fixed straight away. One signs up in stages according to one's level of training.

Presiding Judge I have your Air Force personnel file here. You have consistently received the best appraisals and on each occasion you were, and I quote: 'unreservedly recommended for promotion'.

Defendant What you need to bear in mind is: the proportion of people that apply to join the Air Force who end up in the cockpit of a fighter jet is one in ten thousand. Even out of the trained pilots only one in ten is ever going to fly the Eurofighter.

Presiding Judge So it's a rigorous selection process.

Defendant In this country there are more chairmen of public companies and more heart surgeons than there are fighter pilots.

Presiding Judge Let us come to the events of 26th May. Did you follow the statement made here in the court by the witness Lt Col Lauterbach?

Defendant Yes.

Presiding Judge And in your view, did the witness represent the sequence of events accurately?

Defendant Yes.

Presiding Judge They match your recollections?

Defendant Completely.

Presiding Judge Good. Would you describe for us the minutes before the Lufthansa aeroplane was shot down once again please, from your own personal point of view.

Defendant The diversion and the warning shots produced no reaction from the captain of the Lufthansa aircraft, as you have heard. A couple of minutes later we received the order from the DC not to shoot.

Presiding Judge From the witness, Lt Col Lauterbach?

Defendant Yes, that's right. So there was nothing else we could do other than fly alongside the plane. We repeatedly attempted to make contact. By radio and visually. But without success.

Presiding Judge The witness Lt Col Lauterbach told us that you had questioned the order not to shoot.

Defendant That is correct. I checked twice with the command centre to see whether the order to shoot had not been given after all. I knew that the Lufthansa aircraft was only a few minutes away from the stadium.

Presiding Judge What did you think in that moment?

Defendant That's hard to explain.

Presiding Judge We have time. Please, try.

Defendant You have to understand that our entire training, the complicated selection procedures, the courses, the years of physical conditioning, the appraisals by our superiors and so forth, all of that has just one objective: in the most difficult and testing circumstances we have to hold our nerve. Our job is to assess danger quickly and precisely. That is what we're trained to do.

Presiding Judge I see.

Defendant And while we were flying alongside the Lufthansa aircraft, the worst situation which we can encounter in peacetime occurred. I know every one of us has thought about it hundreds of times. We've discussed amongst ourselves, with our families, our friends, our superiors, our law lecturers. Of course, every pilot hopes he's never going to find himself in this situation.

Presiding Judge It's not a combat mission.

Defendant That's just it. The people on board that Lufthansa plane are civilians, we're supposed to be protecting them.

Presiding Judge But what did you think?

Defendant I considered whether I was disobeying an order. To save tens of thousands of people by killing hundreds of them. If you're asking me what was actually going through my mind in that second . . .

Presiding Judge Yes?

Defendant (*more quietly*) I thought about my wife and my son. Innards.

Presiding Judge Innards?

Defendant That's my word for it.

Presiding Judge Aha.

Defendant I thought about death. That everything in my life was now going to change . . .
That's what I thought.

Presiding Judge Very well. What did you do?

Defendant I slipped back behind the Lufthansa plane. So we were now flying a little behind the civilian aircraft, slightly above it. Then I let go of the Sidewinder. I can't remember shouting into the microphone. I only heard that afterwards. My lawyer played me the tape.
It's strange you forget something like that.

Presiding Judge When you fired – that is, when you activated the Sidewinder – did you know what the consequences would be?

Defendant Did I know I'd be put in prison?

Presiding Judge No. Was it clear to you that by shooting you would destroy the aircraft and kill the passengers?

Defendant Of course.

Presiding Judge What happened exactly?

Defendant When I fired?

Presiding Judge Yes, what happened to the aeroplane?

Defendant The Sidewinder's infrared heat-seeker locked on to the right engine of the civilian aircraft. That is where the missile hit. Precisely. The kerosene in the wing exploded. This made the wing detach itself from the fuselage. Along with the wing it also lost the air current.

Presiding Judge And then?

Defendant The aircraft turned.

Presiding Judge (*surprised*) It flew backwards?

Defendant No, it rotated. It was now flying on its back, so to speak. There's a simple technical explanation. The air current is lost and . . .

Presiding Judge Alright. And then?

Defendant The heat of the explosion had melted off sections of the plane's outer skin. Four passengers slipped out through these openings.

Presiding Judge Precisely four?

Defendant At least four. That's how many I could see. And luggage, bags, that sort of thing. The interior of the aircraft was on fire. The plastic melted. Then the second wing exploded and the plane crashed.

Presiding Judge What did you do?

Defendant We turned around and flew back to base. There we were arrested.

Presiding Judge We?

Defendant Initially, yes, my fellow officer too. I immediately made a statement.

Presiding Judge Good. Let's go back again. Were you able to see the terrorist at all? Could you tell what he was doing?

Defendant No.

Presiding Judge And the other passengers? What did you see?

Defendant What am I supposed to have seen?

Presiding Judge Did the passengers try to enter the cockpit, for example?

Defendant No.

Presiding Judge Did you see whether passengers were standing in the aisle?

Defendant No, I did not see that.

Presiding Judge We know from studying the Black Box – Volume 93, page 122 and following – that the passengers were attempting to break into the cockpit when the plane exploded.

Defendant I didn't see that.

Presiding Judge You acted against the explicit order of your superior.

Defendant Yes, I did.

Presiding Judge Why?

Defendant Because I thought it was right. I wasn't prepared to let 70,000 people die.

Presiding Judge (*turns to the State Prosecutor*) Are there any other questions for Mr Koch? Prosecutor?

State Prosecutor Following on from the Presiding Judge's question: would you have been able to see whether the passengers were attempting to enter the cockpit?

Defendant The plane was on fire.

State Prosecutor Yes?

Defendant I couldn't see anything, everything was full of smoke.

State Prosecutor So you weren't able to see whether the people thrown out of the plane had been sitting in their seats or standing in the aisle or had been in the process of trying to enter the cockpit?

Defendant No.

Defence Counsel Prosecutor, I really don't know where these questions are meant to lead.

State Prosecutor Are you objecting to my question?

Defence Counsel I simply want to know what it is you are asking.

State Prosecutor Either make a formal objection to my question or don't interrupt me any more.

Presiding Judge Please, please. This is a stressful trial.
    Do you want to object to the State Prosecutor's question? At the moment I can't see any reason . . .

Defence Counsel Fine.

State Prosecutor So you can't rule it out?

Defendant What?

State Prosecutor That the passengers had broken into the cockpit at the moment you fired.

Defendant I can't rule it out.

State Prosecutor You can't rule it out. Jolly good.
On another matter . . .

Defence Counsel What do you mean by 'jolly good'? Are we going to comment on all the defendant's answers now?

State Prosecutor Your Honour, please. I can't exercise my right of cross-examination like this.

Presiding Judge Counsel, I must agree with the Prosecutor. If you wish to object to something please do so formally. If not, then please make no further interruption to her questioning.

The Defence Counsel shakes his head but raises no further protest.

State Prosecutor Mr Koch, I too have read your personal file. During your training you took a particular interest in matters of law. In light of this would you be prepared to give more precise reasons for your ruling?

Defendant I gave a lecture to young fighter pilots on the Federal Constitutional Court's ruling. I assume it's in the file.

State Prosecutor Yes, that's right, there is a note of it. Then I ask you what was your understanding of this ruling. What legal conclusions did you . . .

Presiding Judge Prosecutor, now I have to interrupt. You know that we do not debate matters of law with the defendant. We investigate the facts. And they are the basis on which we shall come to a ruling. That was also the reason why I did not ask Mr Koch any further questions . . .

Defence Counsel Excuse me please. Not only do I regard the State Prosecutor's question as admissible, I find it essential. If we are going to determine my client's guilt, then we need to understand his motivation. It is of relevance how Mr Koch considered his own legal position. As we have heard, he took his decision anything but lightly.

Presiding Judge (*to the audience*) Ladies and gentlemen judges, the Defence Counsel points out that his client had considered his legal position and ought to be questioned about this. In this particular case his argument has some merit. We, like all modern states, have a law which is based on guilt. We punish a defendant according to his or her personal guilt. Earlier forms of law took the deed alone to be decisive. Anyone who killed a person would themselves be killed. Why the crime had been committed was irrelevant. Now, however, we want to understand this 'why'. We want to be able to comprehend what can have motivated someone to break the law. Did he kill to enrich himself? Out of jealousy? Out of pleasure in killing? Or did he have entirely different motives, possibly even ones with which we would agree? Our case today is such that the defendant's motives are evidently closely connected to his notion of the law. So we should hear his thoughts.

(*To the State Prosecutor.*) Very well, I shall admit these questions. Prosecutor.

State Prosecutor Mr Koch, if I understand you correctly, you acted quite deliberately contrary to the ruling of the Federal Constitutional Court.

Defendant Yes.

State Prosecutor You know – this is something else you would have learnt in your training – that you may only contravene an order if that order is against the law.

Defendant I am aware of that.

State Prosecutor And you knew that as part of the powers of the state you are bound by the rulings of the Federal Constitutional Court.

Defendant Basically yes.

State Prosecutor Basically?

Defendant I think the Federal Constitutional Court's ruling is wrong.

State Prosecutor Can you explain that to us?

Defendant Yes. The question is whether the killing of non-participants is permissible in an extreme case.

State Prosecutor The Federal Constitutional Court ruled against that . . .

Defendant But the point is that there are 164 passengers on one side and 70,000 spectators in the stadium on the other. When the figures are so disproportionate, it's impossble not to weigh one side against the other.

State Prosecutor If I understand you correctly, you believe that the larger number of spectators in the stadium justifies killing the passengers.

Defendant Yes.

State Prosecutor So you do weigh one life against another?

Defendant No, not one individual life against another individual life. I just believe that it was right to kill a few people in order to save a great many.

State Prosecutor Fine. Do you fundamentally believe that every human life is of equal value?

Defendant Of course.

State Prosecutor However, protecting an individual life may be abandoned if this will save several other lives?

Defendant Yes.

State Prosecutor Would you imagine please a man who is admitted to hospital because he has broken his arm. Apart from this, he is in excellent health. In this hospital there is a whole series of patients urgently awaiting transplants. It is their only hope. According to your argument they would be entitled to kill the man with the broken arm on the spot in order to harvest his organs.

Defendant No, of course not.

State Prosecutor Why not?

Defendant Exceptions can only be made for large numbers of people.

State Prosecutor So four to one's not enough as far as you're concerned?

Defendant No, definitely not.

State Prosecutor I see. Is a hundred to one better? Or a thousand to one? Ten thousand to one, maybe? Where exactly do you draw the line?

Defendant I can't say. One would have to decide case by case.

State Prosecutor Not 'one'. You mean *you* would have to decide case by case.

Defendant Me?

State Prosecutor Yes, you. Isn't it true that with your decision you're putting yourself in what is – to put it pathetically – a God-like position? You alone are now allowed to decide the proportion which is required for someone to carry on living. You dictate who lives and who dies.

Defendant I . . .

State Prosecutor You see, if every human life is of equal value – as you yourself believe – isn't it impossible to weigh lives against each other by number? Wouldn't that go against this principle?

Defendant The passengers on the civilian plane only had a few minutes to live anyway.

State Prosecutor That is an entirely different argument, though.

Defendant The situation is that the plane would have exploded in the stadium. The passengers only had a very short time to live. Even if I had not fired, they would all have been killed.

State Prosecutor Let me ask again: is the length of the life remaining the sole determining factor now?

Defendant Yes.

State Prosecutor In that case you alone are setting the time frame. Your notion is that people with low life-expectancy are no longer worth protecting. How long are you willing to give those people? Five minutes?

Defendant I don't know . . .

State Prosecutor Less?

Defendant I . . .

State Prosecutor Or more? Can those people phone their relatives and say goodbye? A lot of passengers in the New York attacks did that.

Defendant You . . . You've got to see this in practical terms.

State Prosecutor In practical terms?

Defendant I only shot that plane down at the last moment. I couldn't have waited any longer.

State Prosecutor But that doesn't change anything, does it? Think of our example: if the man in hospital hasn't just broken his arm but is mortally ill and only has a few hours to live, then according to your argument, you don't wait for him to die. You can kill him straight away to harvest his organs.

Defendant No, of course not.

State Prosecutor Why not?

Defendant A few hours are very different from a few minutes. And what's more, the mortally ill patient in your example is innocent.

State Prosecutor Innocent? But weren't the passengers just as innocent?

Defendant Not entirely, no.

State Prosecutor You're going to have to explain that.

Defendant The passengers placed themselves in danger by boarding the aircraft.

State Prosecutor Ah.

Defendant Nowadays it is clear to everyone that there's always a risk of being hijacked. Every airline passenger today knows they could become the victim of a terrorist attack. They can see it everywhere – just think of all the security checks you have to go through at the airport. The threat is obvious to everyone.

State Prosecutor So it's your belief then that by buying a ticket, the passengers are consenting to be killed?

Defendant Potentially killed.

State Prosecutor You don't think that's lost all touch with reality? That it's entirely unrealistic?

Defendant It's the way we live now.

State Prosecutor What about the children on the plane?

Defendant Children?

State Prosecutor There were children on the aeroplane. Did they consent to being killed too?

Defendant I . . .
   Yes, their parents did on their behalf.

State Prosecutor Interesting. But – if I were to follow your reasoning – weren't the people in the stadium also taking such a risk?

Defendant I don't understand.

State Prosecutor In the world as you see it everyone is aware of the dangers of being in a place where crowds congregate. On an underground train, for example, or at a rock concert, a fan zone, or in a football stadium. You could go even further and say that anybody who goes to a cinema or a nightclub or a department store is placing themselves in danger and thereby consenting to being killed.

Defendant That's not what I meant.

State Prosecutor So what did you mean?

Defendant Passengers on aeroplanes are in particular danger.

State Prosecutor Well . . .

Defendant You know, you spend the whole time talking about emotions.

State Prosecutor What do you mean by that?

Defendant You need to look at the whole thing differently.

State Prosecutor Do I?

Defendant Those civilians had become part of a weapon. A terrorist weapon. The terrorist had turned that entire plane into his weapon. And that weapon is what I have to fight against.

State Prosecutor Mr Koch, you're an intelligent man. But aren't you getting carried away just now?

Defendant How?

State Prosecutor By doing that is it not the case that you are denying that the passengers are still human?

Defendant I beg your pardon?

State Prosecutor You are turning the passengers into things, into objects, if you claim that they had become part of a weapon.

Defendant But that's what they were.

State Prosecutor Is there anything human left of them as far as you're concerned? Are they still people if we can only see them as part of a weapon? Doesn't being human have to mean a lot more than that?

Defendant Maybe you can afford these nice ideas. But I'm up there, I am responsible. I can't allow myself to reflect on the nature of human existence. I've got to make a decision.

Takes a drink of water.

Presiding Judge Do you need to take a break, Mr Koch?

Defendant No thank you. Prosecutor, if you're going to go this far, let me explain how a soldier has to think. I swore an oath.

State Prosecutor Yes?

Defendant 'To faithfully serve the Federal Republic of Germany and to bravely defend the rights and freedoms of the German people.' I know it off by heart.

State Prosecutor I don't understand the connection.

Defendant That oath means that a soldier must sacrifice his life if it will protect his country.

State Prosecutor That is correct.

Defendant But that means nothing other than the state will weigh the life of a soldier against the dangers threatening the collective. That's how I have always understood the oath at any rate.

State Prosecutor So what are you trying to say then?

Defendant What I am trying to say is that the state does not exclude people being deliberately sacrificed. A sacrifice for the collective, or, if you prefer, for the values of the collective.

And that is how it has been throughout the ages. A soldier has the duty to protect the community as a whole from harm. Even at the risk of his life. So there, too, one life is weighed against another. The life of a soldier against the life of a civilian.

State Prosecutor That's an interesting argument, Mr Koch. But there are two key differences between your duty as a soldier and the state killing innocent passengers.

Defendant Which are?

State Prosecutor Firstly, as a soldier of this country you're not killed by our state but by soldiers of a foreign state. And secondly, Major Koch: you didn't sacrifice yourself – you killed others.

Defendant But I'm not free to choose, either, whether I'm put in deadly danger. I'm forced to do so by obeying orders.

State Prosecutor You volunteered for the service. Nobody forced you. And you knew the risks when you did so.

Defendant Maybe we're being too theoretical here.

State Prosecutor Are we?

Defendant The key thing is something else.

State Prosecutor Well we'd like to hear what that is.

Defendant As a soldier I'm forced to think about threats. How do I protect the population? How do I safeguard our country? That's my job.

State Prosecutor Go on.

Defendant Have you ever thought about what the Federal Constitutional Court's ruling really means?

State Prosecutor Where are you going with this, Mr Koch?

Defendant I mean what it means in practice. For all of us.

State Prosecutor Yes?

Defendant When you're flying up there, training for a combat mission, the only way you can win is if you put yourself in your opponent's position. You have to anticipate what he's going to do.

State Prosecutor I can see that.

Defendant So if you think about the Federal Constitutional Court's ruling, then it'll be obvious to you what terrorists would do.

State Prosecutor Which is?

Defendant It's quite simple: they'll always use innocent people. The moment they do that the state can't defend itself. Don't you understand? The court has made us helpless. We have been left at the mercy of terrorists. The state is capitulating, we've given up.

You have accused me here of killing the 164 people on board. You reproach me for not following this absurd ruling, as it was my duty to do. Well, Prosecutor, you're right. I didn't do that, because that ruling undermines us all. It is the opposite of what I have been trained for.

State Prosecutor Mr Koch, are you still convinced that you acted correctly?

Defendant Yes.

State Prosecutor You believe that the people on that plane had to sacrifice themselves because reasons of state demanded it?

Defendant Yes.

State Prosecutor And you would do it again?

Defendant Yes.

State Prosecutor Is there no other possible course of action?

Defendant None.

State Prosecutor Then, Mr Koch, I have only one more question for you: would you have fired if your wife had been on that plane?

Defendant What?

State Prosecutor Your wife and your son. What if they had been on the plane? Would you have killed them too?

Defendant I . . . I . . .

Defence Counsel What is the point of this question? This is outrageous.

State Prosecutor No, what's outrageous isn't the question, it's your interruptions.

Presiding Judge Please, please.

Defence Counsel I cannot . . .

Presiding Judge Let's calm down, shall we? Counsel, you are aware that it is our task to investigate whether the defendant's statement stands up. Or whether it is simply an assertion. The Prosecutor's question is specifically aimed to do that.

Defence Counsel Possibly. But it is certainly not our job . . .

Defendant Wait. I am not going to ask myself that question. I can't.

State Prosecutor What can't you do?

Defendant Every answer is wrong.

State Prosecutor You're right. Because it's a matter of life. I have no further questions for the defendant.

Presiding Judge Counsel, do you have any more questions for your client?

Defence Counsel No.

Presiding Judge Fine, then you may return to your seat next to your Counsel, Mr Koch.

The Defendant sits down next to the Defence Counsel.

So, if I hear no objections I would now propose to hear the joint plaintiff as a witness.

Defence Counsel and Prosecutor nod.

Mrs Meiser, you are the joint plaintiff in this case and at the same time you are also a witness. We would like to hear you. Please take a seat in the witness's chair.

Mrs Meiser walks to the witness's chair and sits down.

Presiding Judge Mrs Meiser, I'd like to have your personal details for the record. What is your first name?

Meiser Franziska.

Presiding Judge And your age at your last birthday?

Meiser Thirty-four.

Presiding Judge Where do you live?

Meiser In Munich, it's Truderinger . . .

Presiding Judge (*interrupts*) It's alright, thank you, we don't need the address. Munich is sufficient. What is your profession?

Meiser I'm a nurse.

Presiding Judge And are you working at the moment?

Meiser Yes, at the University Hospital.

Presiding Judge Are you related to the defendant by birth or by marriage?

Meiser No.

Presiding Judge Mrs Meiser, as with every witness here, I am obliged to instruct you. You are obliged to tell the truth here, you are not allowed to omit anything or add anything. False testimony in court is punished severely. Do you understand that?

Meiser Yes.

Presiding Judge (*to Stenographer*) Instruction completed.

The Stenographer stamps the record accordingly.

Presiding Judge Mrs Meiser, your husband was one of the passengers who died on board Lufthansa flight LH 2047 . . .

Meiser No.

Presiding Judge No?

Meiser He didn't *die*. They killed him.

Nods in the direction of the Defendant.

Presiding Judge Please tell us about the day it happened. We can pause in the proceedings at any time if you so wish.

Meiser Well, it was like this. That morning my husband rang up and told me when he was coming back. From Berlin. He worked for Siemens. He'd flown to Berlin that morning for a meeting.

Presiding Judge I see.

Meiser I'd just done two night shifts at the hospital. So I had the day off. I was going to pick him up in the car. I used to do that sometimes – you know the airport is such a long way out, a taxi's very expensive. And he doesn't like getting the train. When I got to the airport the arrivals board just said 'delayed'.

Presiding Judge Were you alone at the airport?

Meiser No. What do you mean, alone?

Presiding Judge Had you taken anyone with you?

Meiser Oh, right. No, our daughter was at home. My mother was looking after her.

Presiding Judge So you were alone.

Meiser Yes.

Presiding Judge What happened after you had read on the arrivals board that the flight was delayed?

Meiser Then I got the text.

Presiding Judge The text?

Meiser Yes.

Presiding Judge Mrs Meiser, please. What did the text say?

Meiser Sorry. I'll read it to you. The police confiscated my phone, I still haven't got it back. But I wrote the message down.

She takes a piece of paper out of her handbag and reads it aloud.

'We have been hijacked by terrorists. We're trying to get into the cockpit. Don't be afraid, we will make it. I love you.' That's all, there's no more. Of course I wrote straight back, but there was no answer.

Presiding Judge What did you write?

Meiser I can't remember exactly. I think it was 'Oh God, what's happened?' or something like that.

Presiding Judge Can you tell us the time of the text message?

Meiser Which one?

Presiding Judge From your husband.

Meiser Yes, wait a minute. 19:48 and 12 seconds. I copied it out from my phone.

Presiding Judge When did you copy it?

Meiser Right at the end. When the policeman told me he needed my phone.

Presiding Judge Yes, thank you. In the police notes on page 86, Volume 7 it says your mobile phone was synchronised to a European time-server.

Meiser Excuse me?

Presiding Judge It means that the time on your phone was correct.

Meiser It does that automatically, I think.

Presiding Judge That's what I was saying. What happened after you received the text?

Meiser I immediately showed my phone to a policeman. I told him my husband would never joke about that sort of thing. The policeman was very young, he still had spots, and he turned bright red. I remember that very clearly. He alerted somebody straight away. I was taken to a room somewhere behind the security desks. Everyone was suddenly very agitated, I could tell. And now I stared getting really scared. People were coming in and going out again all the time. In, out. The whole time.

Presiding Judge When did they confirm that the aeroplane had been hijacked?

Meiser They didn't, not to begin with. An older policeman came in and tried to calm me down. But I'm a nurse, you see, I know all about how to talk to patients. And that's exactly what he sounded like. I didn't believe him.

Presiding Judge And then?

Meiser Eventually another policeman came in, together with a woman. The woman wasn't in uniform. The policeman, who was called Haller or Höller or something like that, sat down next to me. He spoke in a very calm voice. But that only made it worse, you know, someone talking calmly like that. He said that the plane had been hijacked and then shot down. And that now they were looking for survivors.

Presiding Judge Who was the woman?

Meiser A psychologist. She asked if I needed help. But I didn't want any help, I had no idea what could possibly help me. My little daughter was at home lying in her bed not knowing about any of it. She was the one I kept thinking about the whole time. Not my husband, but my daughter.

Presiding Judge What did you do?

Meiser What did I do? Nothing.

Presiding Judge What happened next?

Meiser I can't really remember any more. The policeman with the spots took me back to the arrivals hall. He asked me whether I wanted him to take me to my car or if someone would come and collect me. I just wanted to be left alone. I sat down on a bench in the arrivals hall and watched the sliding doors. It was really strange, I couldn't cry. There were loads of police all over the airport, it was complete chaos. I didn't listen to the announcements. I just sat there on the bench. I didn't even call home. I don't know if you can imagine this. I was waiting for him, watching the sliding doors, still believing he was going to come walking through them.

It's so cruel to lose someone suddenly and not be able to say goodbye.

Presiding Judge I think we should take a break now.

Meiser No, please don't. Can I ask something?

Presiding Judge Yes?

Meiser The police never told me: did the passengers get into the cockpit?

Presiding Judge I beg your pardon?

Meiser Did they manage to get into the cockpit?

Presiding Judge We don't know. That was when the plane was shot down.

Meiser But that's important. If they had, they could have stopped the terrorist, couldn't they? Then there would have been no need to shoot the plane down. Would there?

Presiding Judge You went to the police again later?

Meiser No.

Presiding Judge For the court: page 96, Volume 14 in the files. According to the files you were there once more on 4th September?

Meiser Oh, that's what you mean.

Presiding Judge Do you remember now?

Meiser Yes, I got a letter from the police. All the relatives went to Garching. We were taken to a big hall that belonged to the Air Force.

Presiding Judge Indeed. And what was there?

Meiser That's where all their things were, the personal effects from the wreckage. They'd laid them all out on tables, these long metal tables.

Presiding Judge Was anything returned to you there?

Meiser Just his left shoe. It's not that important.

Presiding Judge Perhaps it is. Please, tell us about the shoe.

Meiser I looked at everything in the hall carefully, along with the other people. There were so many things there, suitcases, watches, briefcases and so forth. But nothing of my husband's. Then, right at the end, at the very back in the last row, I found it, his left shoe. It was in good condition, no scratches, no blood, nothing.

You see, my husband had always really looked after his shoes. He always bought expensive shoes, his favourites were horse leather. He said they might be more expensive but they'd last longer. I took his left shoe off the table. I had to sign a form for it. Then they wanted to wrap it up in a bag but I took it just as it was. It sat next to me on the passenger seat all the way home, that shoe.

My daughter's seven, Your Honour. At the funeral she asked me what was in the coffin if Daddy wasn't there.

I didn't know what to say. She's right, we buried an empty coffin. My daughter thought that was really stupid, praying beside an empty coffin. I couldn't pray at all. Later I went and buried the shoe in the woods, on my own. I don't know if that was right, burying the shoe.

I'm sorry, that probably doesn't make much sense to you. I just don't understand.

Presiding Judge Yes, Mrs Meiser.

Meiser It's hard for my daughter. You know, you just can't explain it. She told me she's already forgotten what Daddy used to smell like. His smell.

Presiding Judge Thank you, Mrs Meiser.

Meiser Can I have my phone back? I'd like to have that text, can you understand that?

Presiding Judge Yes, I do understand. Your telephone will be returned to you as soon as the trial has been concluded. We still require it as evidence. I'm very sorry.

Meiser That's what everyone said.

Presiding Judge What?

Meiser 'I'm sorry.' It doesn't mean anything, when people say that.

Presiding Judge I can't give it to you.

Meiser Yes.

Presiding Judge Are there any further questions for the joint plaintiff and witness?

The Prosecutor and Defence Counsel shake their heads.

Mrs Meiser, thank you, you are now discharged as a witness. If you wish, you are welcome to follow the remainder of the trial.

Meiser leaves the room.

Presiding Judge I will now inform you of the defendant's criminal record: there are no entries, Mr Koch has no previous convictions.

If there are no further questions, motions or proposals –

The State Prosecutor and Defence Counsel shake their heads.

– then that completes the evidence. Prosecutor, do you require any time to prepare your closing statement?

State Prosecutor Yes, I will need a short break.

Presiding Judge Fine. Then let's adjourn for twenty minutes. (*Turns to the Guard once again.*) Call everyone again in twenty minutes.

The Presiding Judge stands and leaves the courtroom. At the same time all other members of the court stand.

Interval.

Act Two

The entire court except the Presiding Judge is seated or standing in their places. The Guard walks to the front of the stage.

Guard All those attending the trial please return to the courtroom, the proceedings are about to continue. All those attending the trial please return to the courtroom, the proceedings are about to continue.

The Presiding Judge enters the courtroom, everyone stands up.

Presiding Judge Please be seated.

All sit.

Prosecutor, we will now hear your closing statement.

State Prosecutor *(stands)* Your Honour, ladies and gentlemen judges – I will say right away: the defendant is not a criminal. His actions are far removed from those we usually investigate in this courtroom. He has killed neither his wife nor her lover, he has not robbed, not committed fraud, and not stolen. On the contrary: by the standards of our society Lars Koch has up until now led an impeccable life, he has done absolutely nothing wrong. One cannot find the slightest fault with him. And I can say that I have been impressed by the integrity and seriousness of his thinking. Lars Koch is not a defendant who attempts to explain away what he has done with tales of childhood trauma, psychic disturbance or some other excuse. He is highly intelligent, level-headed, a man who is in a position to distinguish between right and

74

wrong. Indeed he can probably do so better than most people. Everything that Lars Koch did, he did with full awareness, in absolute clarity. He was convinced that it was the right thing to do and he remains so.

Ladies and gentlemen, yes, the Defence Counsel is right. This case does indeed revolve around one single question: are we allowed to kill innocent people in order to save other innocent people? And is it a question of numbers? Can lives be weighed against each other at a point when for the death of one person four hundred others can be saved?

On the spur of the moment we would all probably do just that. It seems the right thing to do. Perhaps we might not be quite sure and it would take some effort to overcome these doubts. But we would weigh things up, just like we do in other areas of our lives. We would consult our consciences. And we would believe we were acting reasonably and fairly, according to the best of our knowledge and our consciences. We would agree with Lars Koch. And so we could end this trial and find him not guilty.

But, as you have already heard, the constitution demands something different from us. The judges of the Federal Constitutional Court have put it in these words: one life must not be weighed against another. Never, not even in great numbers. This makes us pause. And we owe it to the defendant and to the victims to think about this more carefully.

What are the criteria by which we will decide whether the defendant was allowed to kill or not? We are actually deciding according to our consciences, according to our morals, according to our common sense. And there are other words to express this: the former Minister of Defence referred to an 'extra-legal state of emergency'. Some lawyers call it 'natural law'.

However, ladies and gentlemen, the terminology is irrelevant. The meaning is always the same: that we should decide on the basis of ideas which stand above the law, which are greater than the law, ideas therefore, which replace the law. One has to ask: is this wise? I know that each and every one of you believes that you can rely on your own morals and your own conscience. But that is not true.

In 1951 the German philosopher of ethics Hans Welzel described the so-called trolley problem: on a steep mountain railway, a goods train runs out of control. With all its weight it hurtles down the track into the valley heading for a tiny station. Here, a passenger train is waiting. If the goods train keeps going it will kill hundreds of people. Now imagine for a moment that you are in the signal box. You have the opportunity to change one of the points and divert the goods train on to a siding. The problem is that there are five workmen in this siding repairing the track. If you divert the train, you will kill those five workmen but save hundreds of passengers. What would you do? Would you accept the death of those five people as the price to be paid?

Indeed most people would divert the train. And after some consideration we believe that it is the right thing to do.

But if the scenario is changed only slightly, then it immediately becomes much more complicated. In 1976, Judith Thomson, an American moral philosopher, suggested a variant to this example: the goods train is still hurtling down the mountain, but now there are no points that you can change. You are now a bystander, standing on a bridge, watching what is going on. Next to you is an extremely fat man. If he were to fall off the bridge, he would land on the track. He would be run over, but his body would stop the train. Now you can't simply push the man off, he's much too fat and too strong. So you would have to kill him first, with a knife, for example, then you could throw him down. If you did that you could save the passengers. What would you, ladies and gentlemen judges, do now?

Yes, most people would refuse to kill the man. But what has acutally changed? In fact there's just one thing: we would now have to use our own hands. We would have to kill a human being ourselves with our own hands. And we can't do that. Even though there is hardly any difference between the two situations, in our heads everything has changed. In the first case we are prepared to kill five people – but now it's impossible for us to kill only one. Suddenly it no longer seems possible for us to make the right decision. Ladies and gentlemen, we must therefore accept that there is no certainty in moral questions.

We make mistakes, we make them over and over again, it is in our nature – we cannot help it. Morality, conscience, common sense, natural law, extra-legal state of emergency – each one of these terms is suspect, they shift, and it is in their nature that we cannot be certain what the correct course of action is today and whether we will draw exactly the same conclusions tomorrow.

So we need something more reliable than our spontaneous convictions. Something that we can use to judge by at any time and that we can hold on to. Something that provides us with clarity amid the chaos – a guideline which applies even in the most difficult situations. We need *principles*.

And, ladies and gentlemen judges, we have given ourselves these principles. They are our constitution. We have agreed to judge each individual case by it. Every case is to be measured by it and tested by it. By that constitution – not by our consciences, not by our morals and certainly not by any other higher power. Law and morality must be kept strictly separate.

It has taken us a long time to understand: this is the essence of a state based on justice. You all know what a high price we have had to pay for this knowledge. Only what has become law may be binding for all. A true law passed through the complex democratic procedures of our parliament. And that is why laws, even if to some of us they may appear immoral or wrong, remain valid. Our only recourse is to repeal them. And moral views? Regardless of how correct they may appear to us – they bind no one. Only the law and nothing else can do that. And what is more: a 'morally correct' view may never be placed above the constitution. At least not in a functioning democratic state based on justice.

Now you will also be aware that the constitution allows for a right to resist. There may be laws which lead to such intolerable injustice that to apply them would be inhuman. However, ladies and gentlemen judges, we really cannot say that in the case of Lars Koch: this was not about killing a tyrant.

Our constitution is a collection of principles which must always and unreservedly take precedence over morals, conscience and any other notion. And the highest principle of this constitution is human dignity.

Our constitution begins with the sentence: 'Human dignity shall be inviolable.' It isn't at the beginning by accident. That sentence is the most important statement in the constitution. This first article is 'guaranteed in perpetuity'– that means it cannot be amended as long as the constitution is in force. But what is this dignity actually? The Federal Constitutional Court says that dignity means a human being may never be turned into a mere object of action by the state. 'A mere object of action by the state': what does that mean? The idea can be traced back to Kant. Human beings, says Kant, are able to give themselves their own laws and act according to them, and that is what distinguishes them from all other creatures. They recognise the world and they can think about themselves. This makes them subjects and not mere objects, like a stone. Every human being possesses this dignity.

If decisions are made about any person over which they can have no influence, if decisions are made over their heads, then they become objects. And it is therefore clear: the state may never weigh one life against another. And not against a hundred, or against a thousand lives either. Every individual person – and every one of you ladies and gentlemen judges – possesses this dignity. People are not objects. Life cannot be measured in numbers. It is not a market.

Is this only an idea of professors and philosophers? A demand made by Constitutional Court judges who make their judgements far removed from the stresses of our normal lives? No, quite the opposite. The consequences of a decision that ignores human dignity are what you can see here in the case of Lars Koch. Think of the soldiers in the National Situation and Command Centre. If they had all acted according to the constitution, this situation would never have occurred. Because then the stadium would have been evacuated and only a few people would have been in danger. It is up to you, ladies and gentlemen, in your role as judges, to make clear that that is something you will not tolerate. You do not want the constitution to be breached in the way which the former Minister of Defence demanded.

Of course when Lars Koch shot the Lufthansa plane down the stadium was full. It is no fault of his that those soldiers acted in breach of the constitution. But what is relevant to him is the question raised in this trial by the joint plaintiff: could the passengers have overpowered the terrorist? Could they have beaten down the door to the cockpit? How far did they get? Would there have been time? – We don't know. Could the pilot have acted differently? He was facing his own death and that of so many other people. Would he not have been able to lift the plane up at the last moment to save the people in the stadium? – We don't know. Could the co-pilot have knocked the gun out of the terrorist's hand at the last moment? Might everything have turned out alright in the end? – We don't know that either. And why don't we know all this? Because the defendant took a decision. He alone decided that the passengers had to die. He had no order to do so, quite the opposite. He knew that he was acting in defiance of his orders, in defiance of our laws, in defiance of the constitution and in defiance of our courts. Lars Koch was trained to make the correct decision in the most trying circumstances. Before that day he had thought hundreds of times about what he would do. And that is why he must now bear the consequences. Lars Koch, ladies and gentlemen, is not a hero. He killed. He turned people into mere objects in his own hands. He denied them any opportunity to make a decision . . . he took away their human dignity.

It is a terrible thing – the constitution demands a great deal of us, sometimes more than we think we can bear. But it is more intelligent than we are, more intelligent than our emotions, than our anger and our fear. Only if we respect it, if we respect its principles, if we respect human dignity always and everywhere, can we succeed in living together as a free society in an age of terror.

It's true we are under threat from all sides, our state is exposed to the greatest dangers, and the world around us threatens to collapse. But in this situation it is all the more important for us to rely on the principles of a state based on justice. The law is like friendship – it's no use if it's only there for the good times.

The defendant has told you it was right to kill a few people in order to save many of them. But that really would mean that the law is just for the good times – in the bad, the difficult and the dark times we ought to act differently. No. If you find Lars Koch not guilty, you will declare human dignity and you will declare our constitution worthless. Ladies and gentlemen judges, I am certain you do not want to live in a world like that.

I therefore move that the court find the defendant guilty of murder on 164 counts.

Presiding Judge Thank you, Prosecutor.

Counsel, do you need any more time to prepare?

Defence Counsel No.

Presiding Judge Good, then let's hear your closing statement.

Defence Counsel (*stands up*) Ladies and gentlemen, did you hear the State Prosecutor? Did you understand what she was saying? She wants you to find Lars Koch guilty because of a *principle*. Really, that's exactly what she said – you should lock him up for the rest of his life because of a principle. Because of a principle 70,000 people should have died. I don't care what this principle is called – whether you call it 'the constitution' or 'human dignity' or anything else. All I can say is: thank God Lars Koch did not act on principle, instead he did what was right. I could actually finish my plea right now.

However, let us follow the State Prosecutor's reasoning and consider for a moment whether it actually makes sense to act on principle. The same Immanuel Kant to whom the Prosecutor referred, wrote a short essay on principles. This was in 1797. It was entitled: 'On the Presumed Right to Lie out of Love for Mankind'. And do you know what Kant wrote in that essay? Well, I can tell you: a murderer is standing outside your front door with an axe. Your friend has just escaped from this man and run into your house. Now the murderer says he wants to kill this friend of yours and asks if you know where he is. According to Kant, ladies and gentlemen, in this situation you are not allowed to lie because you are *never* allowed to lie. You have to say, 'Of course, Mr Murderer, he's back there sitting on the sofa watching the football on television. Have a nice day.'

I'm not joking. Kant really does demand that. And the State Prosecutor is demanding the same of you: to place a principle above an individual case, to value principles above lives. Principles may be reasonable and perhaps in most cases they may even be correct. But to follow them here – what kind of insanity would that be? I for one would always lie to the murderer because I believe it's more important to save my friends.

And that, ladies and gentlemen, is the central point of these proceedings. Is it right to place the principle of human dignity above saving human lives? Think about that please. Take a step back for a moment and look at the things as they are. Mr Koch saved 70,000 people. To do so he had to kill 164 people. That's all. Is that horrible? Yes, it is appalling, terrifying, shocking. But was there any alternative? No. Lars Koch weighed up the facts and he made the correct decision. Anyone who has any sense at all can, must and will see that no principle in the world can be more important than saving the lives of 70,000 people. Full stop.

Perhaps now – after the State Prosecutor's closing statement – you might feel uncomfortable if you follow your conscience and not some set of principles. I admit that decisions of conscience are complex, but they are possible. Let us look at this matter in isolation. First you should know that the judges of the Federal Constitutional Court only ruled on whether the Aviation Security Law was constitutional or not. The question of whether a soldier would be criminally liable for shooting down a plane was specifically *not* examined by the judges. It's important that you know this – you are the ones who will now make that judgement. Even though the law itself may have been unconstitutional, whether Lars Koch committed a crime is an entirely different question.

I will try to explain the real problem to you. The judges and our constitution see the value of life as being infinitely large. If that is so, then it is impossible to weigh lives against others – simply because you cannot add anything to infinity. One life is already worth as much as a hundred thousand lives.

Even this basic idea seems rather dubious to me and appears to contradict common sense. And there have always been courts which have decided that it was consistent with the law to choose the so-called 'lesser evil'.

In 1841 the ship *William Brown* sank after hitting an iceberg. The lifeboats couldn't carry all the survivors. They would have sunk and nobody would have survived. Alexander Holmes, an able seaman, threw fourteen or sixteen people – they never did work out the exact number – overboard. After they got back to Philadelphia, Holmes was put on trial for what he had done. The court found him guilty but gave him a very lenient sentence. The judges recognised the necessity of choosing a lesser evil over a greater one. Holmes had rescued the majority of the passengers.

Or think of the case that came before an English court in the year 2000. Siamese twins had been joined together from birth. The doctors said that if they remained in that state both of them would soon die. They wanted to separate the children. Separating them would have meant that one of the children would definitely have been killed. The parents did not want this to happen. The matter came to court. The Court of Appeal ruled in favour of the stronger child and allowed the weaker one to be killed. That too, ladies and gentlemen, is nothing other than weighing one life against another. In his written judgement Lord Justice Brooke, who sat in this case, used the example of a pilotless aircraft which is running out of fuel and on course to crash into a city. He decided that the law would allow the passengers who were destined to die to be shot down. And why? Again: it was the *lesser evil*.

The Vice President of the United States, Dick Cheney, declared a few days after 11th September 2001 that it would have been within the law for the planes to be shot down. Why? It was the lesser evil.

Ladies and gentlemen judges, I admit that this idea of choosing the lesser evil is more at home in other jurisdictions. However, and this is what really matters, it is reasonable. We can go on talking for a long time about the concepts of 'human dignity' and 'the spirit of the constitution'. But the world is not a seminar for law students. In fact we find ourselves exposed to greater dangers than ever before. We may see the pictures every day, but we refuse to believe that they could happen to us. We have banished death from our lives, things will carry on peacefully for ever, so we think. It almost seems as if we are never going to die. But we are under threat: our society, our freedom, our way of life. The terrorists have stated their aims a thousand times: they want to destroy us. And what do we do? Have we got anything to oppose them with? Lars Koch has already explained this to you. Think of an attacker, someone who is confused, someone who because of some abstruse ideology or because of some fanatical beliefs, wants to commit murder. All his efforts are geared towards death and destruction. Now this attacker reads about the verdict of the Federal Constitutional Court. What conclusions does he draw? Does he think to himself: oh yes, human dignity, they're right, I better not? That terrorist is going to go down the route those judges have provided. He is going to hijack an aircraft with as many innocent people on board as possible. Then he has a guarantee that our fastidiously just state will do nothing to stop him. The Federal Constitutional Court has given in. Don't you do that, ladies and gentlemen. A guilty verdict for Lars Koch doesn't protect *our* lives: it protects our enemies, the terrorists and the attacks they make on our lives.

Ladies and gentlemen judges, if you find Lars Koch guilty today, if you place a dubious constitutional principle above this individual case, by doing that you will be saying that we are not allowed to defend ourselves against terrorists. Perhaps the State Prosecutor is right, perhaps by doing that we are turning the passengers into objects and perhaps we are taking away their dignity. But we have to understand that we are at war. We did not choose it but we cannot change it. And, even if no one wants to hear this any more nowadays, there cannot be wars without victims.

For these reasons I move for a verdict of not guilty.

Presiding Judge Mr Koch, you are the defendant in these proceedings. The court allows you the last word before retiring to consider a verdict. Is there anything else you would like to say in your defence?

Defendant (*stands up*) I agree with the statement made by my Defence Counsel. Everything has been said.

Presiding Judge Ladies and gentlemen, you have now heard the evidence from the defendant, the witnesses and the closing statements from both the Prosecution and the Defence. You will also bear in mind the defendant's last words as you consider your decision. Now it is up to you alone to reach a just verdict. Do not let yourself be swayed by sympathy or antipathy towards the Defence Counsel or the State Prosecutor. Judge purely on the basis of what you consider to be right. You are now familiar with the arguments for both sides. I believe that the Prosecution and the Defence have each made their positions sufficiently clear. You must decide.

In 155 BC in Rome the Greek philosopher Carneades gave two orations on consecutive days. On the first day he argued the case brilliantly for a series of legal theories.

On the second day he found equally brilliant arguments to reject them all. His listeners were outraged. Yet all Carneades proved was that the truth is not a matter of argument.

Legally, in making your decision you must know the following: there can be no doubt here that the defendant committed the act – even the Defence Counsel has not disputed this. Your deliberations should therefore focus on the question of whether the defendant was allowed to contravene the restrictions placed upon him by the Federal Constitutional Court and the constitution. That is the heart of the matter. It may be that some among you will be minded to convict the defendant though in the light of the special circumstances of this case you do not wish him to have to serve a prison sentence. We judges have no possibility of first convicting the defendant because he has acted illegally and then subsequently pardoning him. That is the responsibility of other offices.

Once you have reached a verdict I shall announce it immediately. You alone will determine the outcome of this trial.

I know that this is a difficult decision but I am confident that you will succeed in judging the case of Lars Koch properly.

The Presiding Judge exits.

The Verdicts

*Depending on the result of the audience's vote the
Presiding Judge announces that the defendant has been
found guilty or not guilty.*

GUILTY VERDICT

Guard All members of the court please return to the
chamber.

*The Defence Counsel, State Prosecutor and Stenographer
take their seats. The Defendant is led in by the Guard
and takes a seat next to the Defence Counsel. The
Presiding Judge enters the chamber. All rise and remain
standing.*

Presiding Judge I declare that the verdict is as follows:
On the charge of murder on 164 counts the defendant
Lars Koch has been found guilty.

Please be seated. I have to announce the following
order:

The arrest warrant made by the county court remains
in force as a result of the defendant being convicted.

*The Presiding Judge signs the order and passes it to the
Stenographer.*

It should be recorded that the verdict is based on the
following: . . . judges voted for a conviction and . . .
judges voted for an acquittal.

For the record: the defendant grew up in a middle-class
family, began school at the appropriate age and after

graduating from high school he completed training as a fighter pilot. He was most recently a Major in the Air Force. His life has been without reproach. He is married and has one son from this marriage.

On 26th May 2013 at 8.21 p.m., using an air-to-air guided weapons system, the defendant shot down a passenger aircraft belonging to Lufthansa German Airlines and did thereby kill the 164 persons on board. I can omit any further details of his actions: they are evident to all of us. The Federal Constitutional Court, as the Defence Counsel has aptly remarked, did not rule on whether this case represents a criminal offence. As to the legal grounds it should be noted:

Our law attaches no blame to a perpetrator who is averting danger from himself, a dependant or another person close to him. So if a father who is driving a car swerves to avoid his daughter and in doing so runs over a cyclist, he is not punished. But there was no such close relationship between Lars Koch and the spectators in the stadium.

So he could only be absolved of blame for a reason which is is not included in law. One possibility might be a so-called 'extra-legal state of emergency.' Indeed former Minister of Defence Jung has already called for this.

Such an extra-legal state of emergency is not regulated by the constitution, the criminal code or any other law. Legal commentaries have doubted whether it even exists.

This court at any rate considers it wrong to weigh one life against another, no matter what the numbers are. To do so contravenes our constitution and breaks the fundamental norms our our common life. Even in extreme situations the constitution must be upheld. Its highest principle – human dignity – may be a construct but that does not mean it is not worth protecting. On the contrary; it is and remains our sole guarantee of being able to live in a civilised community.

We shall illustrate this with an example: on 5th July 1884, an English yacht, the *Mignonette*, was caught in a storm. Some 1,600 miles from the Cape of Good Hope it capsized and sank. The crew was made up of four men: the captain, two strong sailors and a skinny seventeen-year-old ship's boy. They managed to save themselves in a lifeboat. All they had on board were two tins of turnips. They survived on these for three days. On the fourth day they caught a small turtle which they could eat until the twelfth day. They had no water, and they only occasionally managed to catch a few drops of rainwater with their jackets. On the eighteenth day after the storm – by which time they had not eaten for eight days and not drunk for five days – the Captain suggested that one of the men among them be killed in order that the others be saved. Three days later the Captain had the idea of drawing lots – whoever lost, should be killed. But then they remembered that they had families while the boy was an orphan. They rejected the idea of drawing lots. The Captain was of the view that it was better simply to kill the boy. The next morning – with still no rescue in sight – the Captain approached the boy. He lay in a corner of the boat half crazed with thirst. He had drunk seawater and his body was dehydrated. It was clear that he was going to die within hours. The Captain told him his time had come. Then he stabbed him in the neck with a knife.

In the days that followed the three seamen ate parts of the boy's body and drank his blood. On the fourth day after the deed, passengers on a passing ship came across the lifeboat. The three survivors were rescued and brought back to London.

The authorities had the seamen arrested. The Captain came forward as a witness. The case went down in legal history under the title: 'The Queen versus Dudley and Stephens' – that was the name of the two sailors. The sole question at the trial – very similar to our own case – was:

were the seamen allowed to kill the ship's boy in order to save their own lives? Three lives against one? The judge came straight to the point. In his judgement he said:

'The prisoners were subject to terrible temptation, to sufferings which might try the conscience of the best . . . but by what measure is the comparative value of lives to be measured?'

And he went on to say: 'Is it to be strength, or intellect, or what? In this case the weakest, the youngest, the most unresisting, was chosen. Was it more necessary to kill him than one of the grown men? The answer must be "No".'

The judge sentenced the seamen to death for murder but recommended that they be pardoned. They were released after serving six months. The judgement contains some wonderful words which this court stands by to this day, 130 years later:

'We are often compelled to set up standards we cannot reach ourselves, and to lay down rules which we could not ourselves satisfy. But a man has no right to allow compassion for the criminal to change or weaken in any manner the legal definition of the crime.'

The court has no doubt that the defendant made a serious effort and applied the full powers of his conscience to making the correct decision. It is a tragedy that he failed. But we cannot allow this failure to set a precedent.

The passengers on the Lufthansa aircraft were the helpless victims not only of the terrorist but also of Lars Koch. They were killed, their dignity, their inalienable rights, their entire human existence were all ignored. Human beings are not objects. Their lives cannot be measured in numbers. They are not subordinate to the laws of the market. Today's verdict in this court should also be understood as a renewed warning of the terrible dangers created by violating the fundamental values of our constitution.

The defendant has therefore been found guilty.

This trial is now closed. The lay judges are released from their duties with our thanks.

The Presiding Judge rises. At the same time everyone else – except the Defendant – stands up. The Presiding Judge exits via the door behind the judge's bench.

Curtain.

The End.

NOT GUILTY VERDICT

Guard All members of the court please return to the chamber.

The Defence Counsel, State Prosecutor and Stenographer take their seats. The Defendant is led in by the Guard and takes a seat next to the Defence Counsel. The Presiding Judge enters the chamber. All rise and remain standing.

Presiding Judge I declare that the verdict is as follows: On the charge of murder on 164 counts the defendant Lars Koch has been found not guilty.
Please be seated. I have to announce the following order:
The arrest warrant made by the county court can be lifted as a result of the defendant being acquitted.

Presiding Judge signs the order and passes it to the Stenographer.

It should be recorded that the verdict is based on the following: . . . judges voted for a conviction and . . . judges voted for an acquittal.
For the record: the defendant grew up in a middle-class family, began school at the appropriate age and after graduating from high school he completed training as a

fighter pilot. He was most recently a Major in the Air
Force. His life has been without reproach. He is married
and has one son from this marriage.

On 26th May 2013 at 8.21 p.m., using an air-to-air
guided weapons system, the defendant shot down a
passenger aircraft belonging to Lufthansa German
Airlines and did thereby kill the 164 persons on board.
I can omit any further details of his actions: they are
evident to all of us. The Federal Constitutional Court, as
the Defence Counsel has aptly remarked, did not rule on
whether this case represents a criminal offence. As to the
legal grounds it should be noted:

Our law attaches no blame to a perpetrator who is
averting danger from himself, a dependant or another
person close to him. So if a father who is driving a car
swerves to avoid his daughter and in doing so runs over a
cyclist, he is not punished. But there was no such close
relationship between Lars Koch and the spectators in the
stadium.

So he could only be absolved of blame for a reason
which is is not included in law. One possibility might be a
so-called 'extra-legal state of emergency'. Indeed former
Minister of Defence Jung has already called for this. Such
an extra-legal state of emergency is not regulated by the
constitution, the criminal code or any other law. In this
the court recognises a contradiction of values which it is
unwilling to accept: for if a perpetrator acts egotistically,
attempting 'only' to rescue himself or close relatives, the
law absolves him of blame – whereas if he acts selflessly
he is acting against the law. To elevate an egotistical
perpetrator above a selfless one is neither reasonable nor
consistent with the aims of our communal life.

We have no doubt that the defendant made a serious
effort and applied the full powers of his conscience to
making the correct decision. Lars Koch did not shoot
from personal motives, but in order to save the people

in the stadium. He therefore chose what was objectively the lesser evil. For this reason no criminal blame can be attached to him.

The argument of the State Prosecutor that passengers might have been able to force their way into the cockpit or the pilot might have been able to make the aircraft fly higher, is an interesting one but is not ultimately persuasive. For one thing, it cannot be proven. For another, miracles may happen but our duty is not to deal with miracles but with facts. Otherwise it would be impossible to express a verdict. The Prosecution's view that lives which have been given up for lost may not be curtailed further is doubtless correct. But such cases – we think of organ transplants from the dying, for example – are different from this one. This case bears no parallels to the remaining reality of our lives, so that the Prosecution's otherwise correct argument to avoid precedent is not applicable.

To summarise we wish to observe: even though this may be hard to bear, we must accept that our laws are evidently not in a position to solve every moral problem in a manner free from contradiction. Lars Koch became a judge of life and death. We possess no legal criteria to test the decision of his conscience definitively. The law, the constitution and the courts left him alone with his decision. It is therefore our considered view that it is wrong to condemn him for it now.

The defendant has therefore been found not guilty.

This trial is now closed. The lay judges are released from their duties with our thanks.

The Presiding Judge rises. At the same time everyone else – except the Defendant – stands up. The Presiding Judge exits via the door behind the judge's bench.

Curtain.

The End.

'Keep Going Come What May'

A speech given by Ferdinand von Schirach in presenting the M100 Sanssouci Media Award 2015 to Charlie Hebdo

Bonsoir, Monsieur Biard. Good evening, ladies and gentlemen.

On 2nd November 2011 the magazine *Charlie Hebdo* was firebombed. A few days before, a drawing of the prophet Mohammed had been printed on its front cover. Its offices were burnt out, its equipment destroyed and the magazine's website was hacked. This now read: 'God's curse fall upon you.' Next to these words was a picture of the mosque in Mecca.

Barely four years later, on 7th January 2015, at around 11.30 a.m., two masked men force their way into the editorial offices. Journalists, cartoonists and a visitor are sitting around a conference table with a cake on it. It's someone's birthday. The attackers kill eleven people. While on the run through Paris, the murderers shoot in the face a policeman who is lying on the ground. He also dies. Later a third Islamist kills five more people in Paris, including customers of a Jewish supermarket.

These men, the sons of Algerian immigrants, were trained in Yemen by Al Qaeda. And indeed a few days later one of the leaders of that terrorist organisation claims responsibility for the attack. This was the most violent terrorist attack in France since 1961 and seventeen people were murdered. A bloodbath because of a couple of cartoons.

Today this prize honours the dead. And it also honours the survivors. Everyone would have understood if the journalists and artists had not kept going. The fact that you and your colleagues have done so, dear Mr Biard, that

95

Charlie Hebdo still exists, comes despite many things. Despite the murder of your friends, despite the grief you feel for them and despite the conditions under which you now have to work. For this you deserve every prize there is and for this I pay tribute to you.

*

In the discussion that followed the murders of 7th January almost every newspaper in Germany quoted an essay written by the author Kurt Tucholsky in the year 1919. Here Tucholsky had asked, 'What is satire allowed to do?' to which he promptly supplied his own answer: 'Everything.' Arts journalists wrote their pieces, almost every editor composed a leading article and practically all of them agreed with Tucholsky. Their solidarity is understandable – but in fact Tucholsky meant something else entirely.

He wrote those words at a very different time. The First World War had been lost, the Kaiser had fled the country, society had collapsed. Tucholsky's hopes, like those of so many, lay with democracy. This was what he was fighting for as a writer and essayist, and that is why he did not care in the slightest whether the authorities allowed his writings. Quite often they didn't. At the time artists such as George Grosz and Karl Arnold were also charged with criminal offences. What Tucholsky meant was that satire could allow itself to do anything, that artists were disappointed idealists taking on reality.

He only experienced Hitler's regime in its infancy. When he wrote those words, the Nazi magazine *Der Stürmer* did not yet exist. If he had been aware of the outrageous caricatures of Jews it would publish, he would certainly have written those words very differently.

Ladies and gentlemen, cartoons can be art and artistic freedom is now guaranteed in our constitutions. But it is enormously difficult to define what art actually is. In Paris in 1917 Marcel Duchamp placed a urinal on top of a plinth and said that this was art because he declared it was art.

Subsequently Kurt Schwitters and Joseph Beuys would advocate the view that everyone is an artist and everything is art. If that were true and if it were also true that art is entirely free then everyone would be allowed to do everything. That would be the end of our society. 'Strictly speaking, there is no such thing as "art". There are only artists,' said the leading art historian of the twentieth century, Ernst Gombrich. It is a wise statement. Who is doing the drawing and the writing is always important too. Art is what artists do.

Quite apart from this, the issue of how far satire and caricature are allowed to go is one that should never concern a satirical magazine. Satire stays alive by being transgressive. Once it stops doing that, it stops being satire. If everything is allowed, there is no need for it any more. Satire has to be sharp, critical and provocative. It has to hurt and upset people. If it doesn't hurt anyone, it doesn't mean anything. Artists cannot care whether what they are doing is allowed. And now they have no need to care because they no longer have to fear for their lives because in our enlightened society discussions about the limits of art, satire and caricature take place in a courtroom. That is perhaps art's true freedom.

And precisely that was also *Charlie Hebdo*'s story up until the attacks. A few months ago the newspaper *Le Monde* published an article entitled '*Charlie Hebdo*: Twenty-Two Years of Trials'. Indeed the magazine has been sued by practically everyone who could sue – from every possible religious organisation to politicians and journalists. The Catholic Church alone took out fourteen different lawsuits against *Charlie Hebdo* – and lost every one of them. This places the magazine in a long tradition.

One famous trial arising from a cartoon took place in Paris on 14th November 1831. The defendant was Charles Philipon, then thirty-one years old, publisher of various satirical magazines. Philipon owned the largest lithographic publishing house in Paris. He was a republican who was both disappointed and repulsed by the lust for power shown by King Louis Philippe I, who was meant to be a 'Citizen King'. A caricature of the King appeared in one of his newspapers – initially overlooked by the censors – painting over the ideals of the revolution. Philipon was charged with *lèse-majesté* and Heinrich Heine wrote a contemporary account of his trial. Philipon initially argued in court that he had not attacked the King in person but rather 'political power in abstract form' – and that he had a right to do this. The judges shook their heads. Then Philipon said that the charge contravened the freedom of speech and of the press that had been established in 1830. He was wrong. The charter of 1830 – along with the constitution – precluded freedom of speech where the King was concerned. Philipon did not give up. He explained to his judges that if one was determined to recognise the King in one drawing, one could do so in any drawing. And that anyone who drew anything could therefore be accused of *lèse-majesté*.

The judges stared at the defendant with incomprehension. And what Philipon did next was brilliant. He took a piece of paper and drew on it the face of King Louis Philippe, a fat man with soft features and a double chin. And then he altered this face by adding three more sketches, removing it ever further from what it had been – until practically only the shape of the King's head remained. And this was the outline of a pear. So that Philipon was drawing a pear and not the King.

Of course he was found guilty anyway – this sometimes happens, even with brilliant defences – but Philipon published his closing speech and the drawings in the satirical magazines *La Caricature* and *Le Charivari*, and the matter became a great success. The King became widely known as 'the pear' and now all anyone who wanted to criticise the hated July monarchy and the King needed to do was draw a pear.

Today no one risks criminal prosecution for depicting the King or the Federal Chancellor as a piece of fruit any more. The German satirical magazine *Titanic* was the first to apply the same term to Helmut Kohl in 1982. A book was published in 1983 by Pit Knorr, a writer and co-founder of *Titanic*, and illustrated by Hans Traxler entitled *Pear: The Book about the Chancellor. A handbook for up-coming chancers and rotten rascals in this country of ours.* In 1987 the youth wing of Kohl's party adopted this image and even produced a pear-shaped election sticker. Perhaps that is actually the cleverest way to deal with satire. By the way, Helmut Kohl, who has probably had to put up with more insults than any of us, never sued *Titanic* even though he would certainly have won a number of those cases.

A couple of weeks ago the newspaper of the Greek governing party, Syriza, published a cartoon of Wolfgang Schäuble. Its title was: 'The negotiations have begun.' Schäuble was shown in a Nazi uniform. The two speech bubbles said: 'We insist on making soap from your fat' and 'We will only discuss turning your ashes into fertiliser'. This was clearly satire. And it was obvious from Schäuble's spokesman how angry he was. But he said this was freedom of speech. In the latest edition of *Charlie Hebdo* Angela Merkel was depicted in the same uniform. She was pointing stooping Greeks in the direction of a gas chamber and underneath this stood: 'Go in there, that's where your debts will be written off.' And the current cover shows the drowned body of a child refugee on a beach with a billboard in the background carrying a McDonald's ad for 'Two kids' menus for the price of one'. I am convinced that solidarity will soon come to an end and the call 'satire is free' will quickly be forgotten. Yesterday one large German news agency wrote that '*Charlie Hebdo* is losing sympathy'.

Ladies and gentlemen, everyone who is in the public eye – and many people in this room are – is exposed to criticism.

This can hurt or upset anyone. Sometimes that criticism consists of mockery and ridicule, sometimes it is cruel and nasty, sometimes banal and stupid and unfortunately there are times when it can be intelligent and justified. We quarrel with it, write letters, make phone calls, complain to anybody who will listen and ultimately we might even sue in court. But even if it goes way beyond what is allowed, we don't murder our critics and once we have calmed down again we know that they have to exist – even if we can't abide them.

Should the rules be any different for religious communities? I don't think so. I can find no justification for blasphemy to merit any special punishment today. Why should someone's religion receive greater protection from insults than, for example, their sexual orientation, the colour of their skin or their nationality? I believe in the calm, free spirit of our constitution, in its superior tolerance and its benign view of humanity. And that is why I am convinced that religions – just like all other ideas too – may be exposed to criticism. And this is especially true when acts of violence are justified on religious grounds.

But the fundamental issue, ladies and gentlemen, is another one. Modern states came into existence because people were able to refrain from exacting personal justice. They transferred their anger and their need for revenge to the state. They handed in their weapons. The state alone should have the power to punish. It alone should be able to undertake proceedings recognised by all. The term 'monopoly on violence' has been in use since it was coined by the great sociologist of the last century Max Weber, but of course the practice itself is much older. It forms the contract between the citizens and their state, the foundation of our communal life: we refrain from violence and in return we are guaranteed orderly treatment. This was never easy. It took centuries to get this far. The history of this contract is the history of the development of the modern rule of law and it is through this that we became who we are now.

And this is why a terrorist attack cannot be compared with a husband killing his wife or a thief robbing a bank. It is not a breach of the rule of law: it is an attack on the rule of law. We carry out discussions in the newspapers, on television and on the internet supported by our constitution while the terrorists' sole aim is to smash it into pieces. In the face of the reality of terrorism our declaration that 'satire is free' is naive and helpless. We talk about the finely calibrated boundaries of pencil drawings while Islamists' appetite for murder is unsated. Their bloody deeds are not contributions to any discussion and their victims bear no guilt for these acts of personal justice – no matter whether what they did was permitted or not.

And what conclusions do we draw from all of this?

I remain convinced that enlightened democracies can only tackle terrorists, people who want to destroy our society, within the means of the law. This is the only way for a state based on justice to manifest its resilience and integrity. In our anger, in our desire for revenge, we are always in danger of forgetting this. Guantánamo is just one of the terrible examples of what happens when we do so.

But there is another consequence that is harder to measure and less obvious. You will certainly remember that representatives of the governments of almost all free nations declared after the attack that it had not only been an attack on life but an 'attack on freedom of speech and of the press'. Those were the words of Angela Merkel, for example. And that is certainly what was planned. But in reality this terrorist act strengthened freedom of speech more than anything else. Soon after the attack, all over France and the whole of Europe, in Amsterdam, Berlin, Brussels, Lisbon, London, Madrid, Milan, Rome and Vienna, people took to the streets. On 11th January 2015 there were 1.5 million people in Paris and over 3.7 million across the country. One commentator observed that this was more people than had ever demonstrated together in France in support of a single cause since the French Revolution. Many of them carried banners with the words 'Je suis Charlie'. They mourned for the dead and they demonstrated for the right to freedom of expression. I don't think a basic right has ever had so much support.

That some of the staff of *Charlie Hebdo* left the magazine after the attacks is only too understandable. And the fact that other journalists no longer dare to express themselves freely about Islam is shocking. Perhaps prizes like this one can offer them some support.

However, the more profound truth is that it is not terrorists who will destroy our society. They cannot do that. We ourselves, ladies and gentlemen, are the only ones who can seriously endanger our values. Only we, the democrats, can damage democracy. And that can happen quickly. The populists are now on the rise. Politicians are demanding tougher laws and the secret services greater powers. Parties everywhere talk of a 'threat of the Islamisation of Europe' and feel 'vindicated' by the attacks in Paris. There are demands for a database of suspicious persons and intensive surveillance of the internet. This is the real effect of terrorism, one that is indirect and therefore dangerous.

A few weeks ago I was queuing at Zurich airport behind a very elegant lady who was around ninety years old. She appeared a little confused and unable to cope with the situation. Her hand baggage was checked, she had to take off her shoes and her body was patted down. I could see how unpleasant she found it all. In her handbag there was a small bottle of perfume. The security guard said she had to put it in a plastic bag. Of course the old lady didn't have one with her. The guard wanted to take the bottle away from her. And then something unusual happened. The other passengers began to protest. They got quite loud and in the end the guard hesitantly returned the lady's perfume. The terrorists, ladies and gentlemen, have nearly won already. We need to be careful.

It is silly to believe that the state is defenceless against terrorism. But neither war cries nor acts of blind rage are any use to us now. It is only prudence, only the constitution, only the rule of law that can provide us with lasting protection. If we betray the rules we have given ourselves, we will lose. On 22nd July 2011 Anders Breivik murdered seventy-seven people in Norway, including thirty-two children and young people, out of completely insane pseudo-political motives. But afterwards Norway passed no new surveillance laws and did not set up body scanners outside schools and holiday camps. Prime Minister Stoltenberg did the opposite. At the memorial service in Oslo Cathedral he said: 'We will never give up our values. Our response is: more democracy, more openness, more humanity. We will show the world that democracy gets stronger when most depends on it.' Stoltenberg's words moved me a great deal at the time and they still do now. They are the core of what should matter to us. We must confront fanatics with what they fear and hate most of all: our tolerance, our sense of humanity, our freedom and our laws.

Tucholsky died in 1935. Erich Kästner would later describe him as the 'short, fat Berliner who tried to avert a catastrophe with a typewriter'. But do you know, ladies and gentlemen, what drove him, just like his role model Heinrich Heine and later Stefan Zweig, Elias Canetti, Thomas Mann and so many others to criticise their countries? It was not malice, hatred or wilful destruction. It was the opposite. To put it in one word – one that might be too pathetic by today's standards – it was their profound love of freedom, of the wonderful richness of life. Or, in more modern terms, their conviction that we should live only in an enlightened, nuanced and liberal society.

Recently I spent a while watching the Christopher Street Day parade. A tall, incredibly beautiful black man was dancing in the street. He was naked apart from an awfully tight pair of briefs and the white angel wings he wore on his back. Passers-by stared at him. A short Arab man was standing by the kerb with his wife and child. He was no more than five feet two inches tall, bearded and rather hunched. As the dancer approached the Arab, I thought: this is not going to go well. He stopped in front of him, bent down, took his face in both hands and kissed him on the mouth. The Arab went red, but then he beamed and chuckled silently.

The world we live in is not perfect, but it is better than in previous centuries. And in this world we need *Charlie Hebdo*, and we need you, Monsieur Biard. Your magazine is irreverent and flippant and angry and every now and again it is insufferable. It often oversteps the mark of what is allowed. But this makes it an expression and representation of our liberty. It is part of the world that was created through so many centuries of struggle, repression and pain. No one in their right mind can want us to retreat back behind the Enlightenment once again, and Benjamin Franklin's warning is even more pertinent now than it was in his own time: 'If we restrict liberty to attain security we will lose them both.'

Dear Monsieur Biard, we therefore ask you to keep going with *Charlie Hebdo*. Keep going come what may, keep doing exactly what you are doing for as long as you possibly can.

FERDINAND VON SCHIRACH